ASK * ME
ANYTHING
ABOUT * THE
PRESIDENTS

LOUIS PHILLIPS, the author of over two dozen books for children and adults, has been collecting facts about the presidents since fourth grade. His love for odd and unusual information has remained with him until this day. Other books by the author include *The Million Dollar Potato, Wackysaurus,* and the upcoming *Alligator Wrestling and You.*

Mr. Phillips lives in New York City with his wife and twin sons.

ASK * ME ANYTHING ABOUT * THE PRESIDENTS

LOUIS PHILLIPS

Illustrated by Valerie Costantino

AN AVON CAMELOT BOOK

ASK ME ANYTHING ABOUT THE PRESIDENTS is an original publication
of Avon Books. This work has never before appeared in book form.

AVON BOOKS
A division of
The Hearst Corporation
1350 Avenue of the Americas
New York, New York 10019

Copyright © 1992 by Louis Phillips
Interior illustrations by Valerie Costantino; copyright © 1992 by Avon Books.
Presidential portraits are from the collections of the Library of Congress
Published by arrangement with the author
Library of Congress Catalog Card Number: 91-90785
ISBN: 0-380-76426-1
RL: 6.7

First Avon Camelot Printing: February 1992

CAMELOT TRADEMARK REG. U.S. PAT. OFF. AND IN OTHER COUNTRIES, MARCA REGIS-
TRADA, HECHO EN U.S.A.

Printed in the U.S.A.

OPM 10 9 8 7 6 5

for Ian and Matthew Phillips

*May you always experience delight
in learning new things*

Do You Know?

Which presidents were not even born in the United States?

Which president never went to school?

Which president had an artificial jaw made of rubber?

Which president refused to shake hands with White House visitors?

Which president did not even vote in his own election?

Which president once wore women's high-button shoes to school?

Which president kept live bears on the White House grounds?

Which president's wife did not attend her husband's inauguration?

What is the text of the Gettysburg Address?

Which president, when he wrote his autobiography, did not mention, even once, his wife's name?

Which president helped save his campaign because he was a good speller?

Has any wife of a president ever been accused of being a spy?

The answers to all these questions and more can be found inside . . .

Who was the first child to be born to a president in the White House?

Born on September 9, 1893, Esther Cleveland, the second child of President and Mrs. Grover Cleveland, was the first child of a president to be born in the White House. Esther Cleveland, however, was not the first child to be born in the White House. That honor goes to a grandson of Thomas Jefferson. James Madison Randolph, son of Thomas Mann Randolph and Martha Jefferson Randolph (daughter of the president), was born in the White House on January 17, 1806.

Which president loved jelly beans so much that his frequent eating of the candies increased their popularity and sales?

Ronald Reagan

Which president invented the revolving (or swivel) chair?
Thomas Jefferson, the greatest of our presidential inventors. In addition to the revolving chair, Jefferson invented a pedometer, a machine to make fiber from hemp, and a letter-copying press. He is also credited with inventing the lazy susan.

Who was the only president to have two vice presidents die while in office?
James Madison. His first vice president, George Clinton, died in office on April 20, 1812. Madison's vice president for his second term was Elbridge Gerry, who died on November 23, 1814.

Has the United States ever had two presidents at the same time?
Technically speaking, yes. Grant and Hayes, for one day. Because March 4, 1877 fell on a Sunday, the first oath of office was administered in private to Hayes. The formal inauguration, however, did not take place until Monday, March 5. Therefore, in a sense, the United States had two presidents on that Sunday in March.

When does the president officially take office?
In the twentieth century, the newly elected president officially takes office on January 20 of the year following his election.

Which president refused to shake hands with all White House visitors?
George Washington. While he was president, instead of shaking hands, he bowed. Washington aristocratically believed that shaking hands was beneath the dignity of a president.

George Washington

1st President

Born: February 22, 1732, in Pope's Creek, Virginia.

Father: Augustine Washington.

Mother: Mary Ball Washington.

Married: Martha Dandridge Custis on January 6, 1759.

Religion: Episcopalian.

Political party: Federalist.

Term of office: April 30, 1789 to March 3, 1797.

Died: December 14, 1799.

Sidelight: Washington was actually born on February 11, but, in 1750, Great Britain changed from the Julian calendar to the Gregorian calendar, and eleven days were omitted from the month of September 1752. To compensate for this omission, eleven days were added to the remaining dates. Washington's birthday then changed from February 11 to February 22.

Did George Washington really wear false teeth made out of wood?

No. For more than 150 years it was rumored that Washington's false teeth had been carved from wood, but Washington's dentures were really made out of such materials as cow's teeth, lead, hippopotamus teeth, carved elephant and walrus tusk, and even other human teeth. The source of the above information is Dr. Reidar Sognnaes, the founding dean of UCLA's School of Dentistry. Some of the human teeth used in creating Washington's dentures most likely were taken from Washington's own mouth.

Dr. Sognnaes, after studying six surviving sets of Washington's false teeth, also concluded that the president's famous pout was probably caused by the fact that denture adhesive hadn't yet been invented. The false teeth were, in fact, held in place by two springs that pushed them up and forward.

Dr. Sognnaes also stated that when Washington became president at age fifty-seven, he had, because of gum disease, but one tooth left. A hole cut in the ivory base of his dentures allowed his one remaining tooth to poke through.

Has any person been president for only one day?

Technically speaking, perhaps. The person in question is David Rice Atchison. On his monument in Missouri, the following words are carved: "David Rice Atchison, 1807–1886, President of the U.S. one day."

How Mr. Atchison's very brief moment of glory came about is as follows. In March 1849, Zachary Taylor was to be sworn in as president, but because the official inauguration day fell on a Sunday, the actual inauguration did not take place until Monday, March 5. James K. Polk's official term as president had ended, according to the Constitution, on noon of March 4. Thus, neither Taylor nor Polk was president from noon, March 4, until the inauguration on Monday, March 5.

In addition, Polk's vice president, George Dallas, had already resigned as president of the Senate, so, David Rice Atchison, from Missouri, was elected by his fellow senators to fill Dallas's place pro tempore. Therefore, Atchison was the acting president for one day.

And what did he do on that Sunday in question? He slept. He slept the day away—the only president who slept through his entire term in office.

Which former president, writing in *Ladies' Home Journal* in 1905, stated that "sensible and responsible women do not want to vote. The relative positions to be assumed by men and women in the working out of our civilization were assigned long ago by a higher intelligence than ours."

Grover Cleveland. History, however, has proved him to be wrong.

What famous pirate was granted a pardon for his crimes by President James Madison?

Jean Laffite (c. 1780–c. 1826). During the War of 1812, the British attempted to get Laffite to fight on their side and to aid them in their attempt to capture New Orleans. Laffite refused and offered to fight for the United States. Laffite and his crew took part in the Battle of New Orleans.

After being pardoned by Madison, Laffite reverted to his old ways and became a pirate once again.

How many presidents died in the White House?

Although eight presidents have died in office, only two presidents died in the White House itself. William Henry Harrison died in the Executive Mansion on April 4, 1841, just one month after his inauguration. Zachary Taylor died in the White House on July 9, 1850.

Who was the first Catholic to become president?
John F. Kennedy

Who was the first president to live in the White House?
John Adams. When Adams and his family moved into the White House (in November 1800) it was still unfinished, and the freshly painted walls were still wet. Mrs. Adams ended up using the East Room as a place to hang her wash.

John Adams

2nd President

Born: October 30, 1735, in Braintree, Massachusetts.
Father: John Adams.
Mother: Susanna Boylston Adams.
Married: Abigail Smith on October 25, 1764.
Religion: Unitarian.
Political party: Federalist.
Term of office: March 4, 1797 to March 3, 1801.
Died: July 4, 1826.
Sidelight: John Adams was the first president to be defeated for reelection.

7

Which president lived through all the presidential administrations from George Washington's through Abraham Lincoln's?

James Buchanan, who lived from 1791 to 1868.

Which president carried a bullet in his arm for nearly twenty years?

Andrew Jackson. Jackson had taken part in a duel in 1812 and was wounded by a man named Jesse Benton. The bullet remained in Jackson's arm until 1832, when it was removed by a surgeon.

Which president ordered the grooms who worked in his stables to brush the teeth of his six white horses every morning?

George Washington

Which president wrote a book about fishing—*Fishing for Fun?*

Although Chester A. Arthur might have been the most expert of our fishing presidents (Eisenhower also loved the sport), Herbert Hoover was one who took the time to write a book on the subject. In *Fishing for Fun,* Hoover tells his readers, "When you get full up of telephone bells, church bells, office boys, columnists, pieces of paper and the household chores—you get that urge to go away from here. Going fishing is the only explanation in the world that even skeptics will accept."

Perhaps the most famous blooper or slip of the tongue ever to occur on radio happened when the well-known announcer Harry Von Zell was introducing which president?

Harry Von Zell, when he introduced Herbert Hoover, said: "Ladies and gentlemen, the President of the United States, Hoobert Heever."

What is the origin of the word "president"?

The word "president" comes from the Latin *praesidens,* present participle of *praesidere,* meaning to preside. To preside is to hold a high position of authority.

Which president, while dedicating the Washington Monument, suffered sunstroke and died five days later?

Zachary Taylor. After standing in the hot sun, he returned to the White House and ate a large bowl of cherries and drank a pitcher of milk. He developed severe cramps, and was diagnosed as suffering from cholera morbus. Five days later he was dead.

Which president was once described as follows: "He is like a singed cat—better than he looks"?
Calvin Coolidge

Which president suffered from migraine headaches that were so severe that the pain would continue for five to six weeks?
Thomas Jefferson. Ulysses S. Grant also suffered from migraines. Being president is, to say the least, a highly stressful job.

Thomas Jefferson

3rd President

Born: April 13, 1743, in Shadwell, Virginia.

Father: Peter Jefferson.

Mother: Jane Randolph Jefferson.

Married: Martha Wayles Skelton on January 1, 1772.

Religion: No formal affiliation.

Political party: Democratic-Republican.

Term of office: March 4, 1801 to March 3, 1809.

Died: July 4, 1826.

Sidelight: He was the first president to be inaugurated in Washington, D.C.

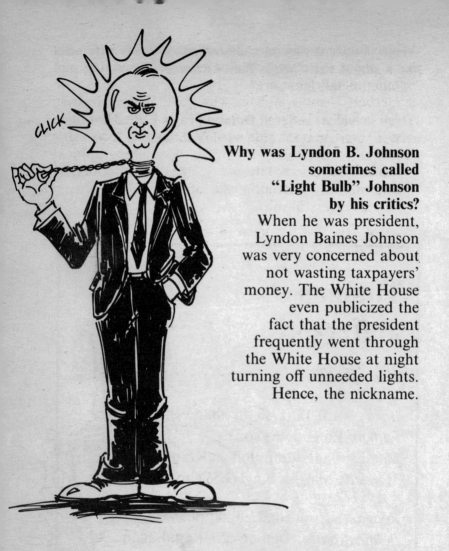

CLICK

**Why was Lyndon B. Johnson
sometimes called
"Light Bulb" Johnson
by his critics?**
When he was president,
Lyndon Baines Johnson
was very concerned about
not wasting taxpayers'
money. The White House
even publicized the
fact that the president
frequently went through
the White House at night
turning off unneeded lights.
Hence, the nickname.

**Which future president served in the Third Fleet in the
South Pacific during World War II and almost lost his
life when, on December 18, 1944, a typhoon struck and
killed 800 men?**
Gerald R. Ford

Which future president collaborated with his wife on a book about metallurgy, the science of extracting and refining metals from ore?
Herbert Hoover and his wife, Lou Henry Hoover, published a 640-page book called *De Re Mettallica* in 1912. The book was a translation of a 1556 work by Georg Agricola (1494–1555), with a biographical introduction, annotations, and an appendix on the development of mining methods.

Who was the last president to wear a beard?
Benjamin Harrison

Which president was so uninterested in clothes that it was said he wore the same hat for ten years?
John Quincy Adams

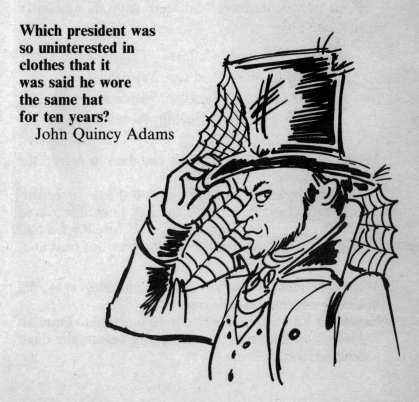

Which presidents were not even born in the United States?
The question is a trick one, based upon a technicality. Eight presidents were, in fact, born not in the United States, but in the thirteen original colonies before they became the United States.

The eight are: Washington, Adams, Jefferson, Madison, Monroe, John Quincy Adams, Andrew Jackson, and William Henry Harrison.

Which presidents have had state capitals named in their honor?
Four presidents have had state capitals named in their honor:

Thomas Jefferson—Jefferson City, Missouri
James Madison—Madison, Wisconsin
Andrew Jackson—Jackson, Mississippi
Abraham Lincoln—Lincoln, Nebraska

Which president fought at least one duel to defend the honor of his wife?
Andrew Jackson. Jackson married the divorcée Rachel Donelson Robards, but they later discovered that the marriage had taken place before Rachel had been officially divorced from her previous husband.

Which president, when he wrote his autobiography, did not even mention his wife once?
Martin Van Buren. He had been married to Hannah Hoes Van Buren for twelve years before she died. They had four sons.

Which president is known as the "Father of the Constitution"?

James Madison, because he contributed many important ideas to the shaping of that document and because he worked so diligently to bring about its ratification.

James Madison

4th President

Born: March 16, 1751, in Port Conway, Virginia.

Father: James Madison.

Mother: Eleanor Rose Conway Madison.

Married: Dorothea (Dolley) Payne Todd on September 15, 1794.

Religion: Episcopalian.

Political party: Democratic-Republican.

Term of office: March 4, 1809 to March 3, 1817.

Died: June 28, 1836.

Sidelight: Madison was the first president who had prior service as a congressman.

Who was the only president to marry the same woman twice?

Andrew Jackson. He married Rachel Donelson Robards in August 1791 in Natchez, Mississippi, but afterwards there was some question whether or not Mrs. Robards had been officially divorced from her first husband, Captain Lewis Robards. Indeed, the divorce proceedings had not been completed, and many people in Washington society were scandalized over the fact that Jackson had married a woman whose divorce had not been finalized. The divorce decree was not final until 1793. Jackson, therefore, married Rachel once again, on January 17, 1794, in Nashville, Tennessee.

Who was the first president to appoint a woman to the United States Supreme Court?
Ronald Reagan. In 1981, he appointed Sandra Day O'Connor as the first woman justice of the Supreme Court.

Which president entered the college of William and Mary when he was only sixteen years old?
James Monroe

James Monroe

5th President

Born: April 28, 1758, in Westmoreland County, Virginia.

Father: Spence Monroe.

Mother: Elizabeth Jones Monroe.

Married: Elizabeth Kortright on February 16, 1786.

Religion: Episcopalian.

Political party: Democratic-Republican.

Term of office: March 4, 1817 to March 3, 1825.

Died: July 4, 1831.

Sidelight: Monroe was the first president to ride on a steamboat.

Newspaper editor William Allen White once said of this president that shaking hands with him was like shaking a "ten-cent pickled mackerel wrapped in brown paper." To what president was he referring?

Woodrow Wilson

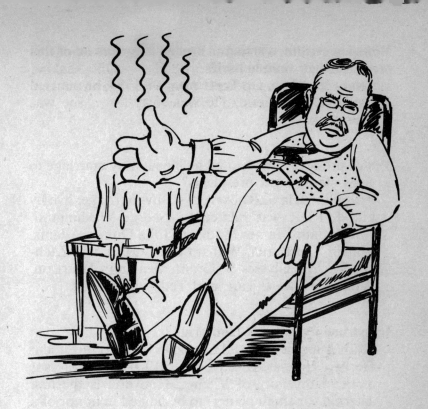

While we're on the subject of handshaking, how many hands did President Theodore Roosevelt shake at a White House New Year's Day celebration in 1907?
On the day in question, Teddy Roosevelt—and you may find this difficult to believe—shook the hands of 8,513 people. Now that's a lot of handshaking.

Was Abraham Lincoln or George Washington our tallest president?
Lincoln, standing at six feet, four inches, has been the tallest president so far.

Which president married a woman who was seventeen years younger than himself?

James Madison. On September 15, 1794, he married Dolley Payne Todd. He was forty-three, she was twenty-six.

Which president was related by blood or by marriage to at least eleven other presidents?

Franklin Delano Roosevelt; six by marriage, five by blood. FDR was related to George Washington, John Adams, James Madison, John Quincy Adams, Martin Van Buren, William Henry Harrison, Zachary Taylor, Ulysses S. Grant, Benjamin Harrison, William Howard Taft, and Teddy Roosevelt.

In astronomy, what is Hooveria?

Hooveria is an asteroid named in honor of President Herbert Hoover. Discovered in 1920 by a professor at the University of Vienna, Hooveria is the first asteroid (or small planet) to be named in honor of a United States president.

George Washington was the only president ever to receive a unanimous vote from the Electoral College—and only one other president received every electoral vote but one. Who was that?

James Monroe. In the 1820 election, Monroe was elected president by the electoral vote of 231 to 1. The only vote cast against Monroe was by a New Hampshire delegate. That delegate voted for John Quincy Adams so that Washington might retain the honor of being the only president to receive unanimous acclaim.

Which president described himself as follows: "I am a man of reserved, cold, and forbidding manners"?
John Quincy Adams

John Quincy Adams

6th President

Born: July 11, 1767, in Braintree, Massachusetts.

Father: John Adams.

Mother: Abigail Smith Adams.

Married: Louisa Catherine Johnson on July 26, 1797.

Religion: Unitarian.

Political party: Democratic-Republican.

Term of office: March 4, 1825 to March 3, 1829.

Died: February 23, 1848.

Sidelight: He named one of his sons George Washington. George Washington Adams was born in Berlin, Germany, in 1801, and died at the age of twenty-eight, an apparent suicide.

Which presidential family was nicknamed the "Three Musketeers" by the White House Staff?

Bess, Margaret, and Harry Truman. They received that nickname because the three liked to be together so much.

Who was the first president to wear long trousers?

When they were in office, George Washington, John Adams, and Thomas Jefferson all wore knee breeches. In the last decade of the eighteenth century, however, long trousers began to make their appearance in America. James Madison, who was inaugurated president in 1809, adopted long trousers, and he was the first president to wear them daily.

Who is the only president to kill a man in a duel?
Andrew Jackson. Jackson, in fact, is believed to have taken part in many duels, but in a duel on May 30, 1806, Jackson shot and killed Charles Dickinson. The men had engaged in the duel because Mr. Dickinson had made some unflattering remarks about Jackson's wife.

Andrew Jackson

7th President

Born: March 15, 1767, in Waxhaw, South Carolina.

Father: Andrew Jackson.

Mother: Elizabeth Hutchinson Jackson.

Married: Rachel Donelson Robards in August 1791 and in a second ceremony on January 17, 1794.

Religion: Presbyterian.

Political party: Democratic.

Term of office: March 4, 1829 to March 3, 1837.

Died: June 8, 1845.

Sidelight: First president to be born in a log cabin.

Which president frequently recited the following limerick about himself:

> *For beauty I am not a star;*
> *There are others more handsome by far.*
> *But my face, I don't mind it,*
> *For I am behind it,*
> *It's the people in front that I jar.*

Woodrow Wilson recited that limerick, so often that he was assumed to have written it. But some editors credit it to Anthony Euler instead.

Which president was a skilled amateur violinist?
Thomas Jefferson. He was also a very good singer.

Which presidents changed their names?

Six presidents adopted names that were different from the names given to them at birth:

Ulysses Simpson Grant—changed from Hiram Ulysses Grant

Grover Cleveland—changed from Stephen Grover Cleveland

Woodrow Wilson—changed from Thomas Woodrow Wilson

Calvin Coolidge—changed from John Calvin Coolidge

Dwight David Eisenhower—changed from David Dwight Eisenhower

Gerald R. Ford—changed from Leslie King, Jr. Gerald Ford changed his name when his mother remarried, and his stepfather legally adopted him.

When former President Tyler died, why was no official announcement of his death made by the U.S. government?

John Tyler, when he died on January 18, 1862, had been elected to the Confederate House of Representatives, and thus was considered to be a rebel by the Union.

Who was the first president born in the nineteenth century?

Franklin Pierce, born November 23, 1804. Millard Fillmore was born on January 7, 1800, but the nineteenth century did not officially begin until January 1, 1801 (all centuries officially start in the 01 year).

Which future president appeared as a model on the cover of _Cosmopolitan_ magazine in 1942?
Gerald R. Ford. He also posed in winter clothes for _Look_ magazine in March 1940.

When Lincoln delivered his Gettysburg Address what disease was he suffering from?
A mild case of smallpox, which was not diagnosed by his physician until Lincoln had given his speech and returned to Washington.

Which future president, during the election of 1789, was so disappointed at receiving only thirty-four electoral votes (out of a possible sixty-nine) for the office of vice president that he seriously considered turning down the office?
John Adams. He was deeply hurt that more than half of the electors did not consider him good enough to be vice president (sixty-nine votes had been cast for Washington, who became president, and the other sixty-nine electoral votes were split among eleven other candidates). He felt it was a stain upon his character, and for a time he thought he should decline the office. Fortunately for the United States, he changed his mind.

Which president once wore women's high-button shoes to school?
Jimmy Carter. When Jimmy was in high school, his father (who owned a supply store) ordered a large number of women's high-button shoes. He had more shoes than he could possibly sell, and so he made all the members of his family wear them— including Jimmy.

Which president kept live bears on the White House grounds?

Thomas Jefferson kept bears on the White House grounds so that passersby could view them. The bears were grizzlies brought back by Lewis and Clarke from their famous expedition. The bears were kept in cages, and for years afterward the White House was sometimes referred to as the "president's bear garden."

"There is no place I should like to see so much as Jerusalem." These were the final words of which president?

Abraham Lincoln

When this president died, the citizens of France were ordered to observe ten days of mourning. Who was the president so honored?

George Washington. He was so popular among the French that when he died, Napoleon Bonaparte ordered ten days of mourning.

27

Who was the first president to issue a pilot's license?

George Washington. In January 1793, when a Frenchman named Jean Pierre Blanchard journeyed to Philadelphia to make an ascent in his hot air balloon (the first balloon flight in United States history), President George Washington joined the crowd to watch the takeoff.

Fearing that people might be alarmed by the sight of a man floating through the air, Washington presented Blanchard with a paper giving him permission to land and urging U.S. citizens not to hinder Blanchard, but to "receive and aid him with humanity and good will, which may render honor to this country." Blanchard flew from Philadelphia to Glouster County, New Jersey, a distance of fifteen miles, in forty-six minutes—and landed safely.

Who was the first president to be born a U.S. citizen?
Martin Van Buren, who was born in 1782, six years after the signing of the Declaration of Independence. All previous presidents had been born when the United States was an English colony.

Martin Van Buren

8th President

Born: December 5, 1782, in Kinderhook, New York.
Father: Abraham Van Buren.
Mother: Maria Hoes Van Buren.
Married: Hannah Hoes on February 21, 1807.
Religion: Dutch Reformed.
Political party: Democratic.
Term of office: March 4, 1837 to March 3, 1841.
Died: July 24, 1862.
Sidelight: Because he was skilled in attaining his political goals, he was nicknamed the "Little Magician."

Which presidential nominee was several days late in officially acknowledging his nomination because he had refused to pay the ten cents postage due on the formal letter of notification?

Zachary Taylor

French President Georges Clemenceau said of this president, "He thinks he is another Jesus Christ come upon the earth to reform men." To whom was Clemenceau referring?

Woodrow Wilson

Which future president sometimes would have a cucumber soaked in vinegar for breakfast?

Ulysses S. Grant sometimes ate such a breakfast when he was general during the Civil War.

What state was originally given the name Jefferson, in honor of the third president?

Colorado was originally incorporated under the name Jefferson.

Who served the shortest term of any president?

William Henry Harrison. He served only thirty-two days, from March 4, 1841, to April 4, 1841.

William Henry Harrison

9th President

Born: February 9, 1773, in Berkeley, Virginia.

Father: Benjamin Harrison.

Mother: Elizabeth Bassett Harrison.

Married: Anna Tuthill Symmes on November 25, 1795.

Religion: Episcopalian.

Political party: Whig.

Term of office: March 4, 1841 to April 4, 1841.

Died: April 4, 1841.

Sidelight: Only president who studied to become a doctor.

Before becoming president, Ronald Reagan was a well-known television performer. What two TV shows did he host?
Ronald Reagan acted as the host for *General Electric Theater* (1954–1962) and for *Death Valley Days* (1962–1965).

GIDDYAP!

DEATH VALLEY DAYS

Which president did not see a map of the United States until he was nineteen years old?
Millard Fillmore. The thirteenth president grew up in a home that had only one book in it—a family *Bible*.

Which president was buried with a copy of the U.S. Constitution placed under his head as a pillow?
Andrew Johnson, who died on July 31, 1875.

Did any presidents ever own slaves?
Yes. Ten of them, in fact, including Washington and Jefferson. In the election of 1844, opponents of James K. Polk unfairly claimed and tried to smear him with the rumor that he had branded his initials on the shoulders of forty-three slaves.

32

Which president had a brother who was nicknamed "Moon"?

Ronald Reagan. His older brother, Neil, had that nickname. When Ronald Reagan was growing up, his nickname was "Dutch."

Which ex-president was so down on his luck that five years after leaving office he was not able to pay a bill for $1.25 until he sold his corn crop?

John Tyler

John Tyler

10th President

Born: March 29, 1790, in Greenway, Virginia.

Father: John Tyler.

Mother: Mary Marot Armistead Tyler.

Married: Letitia Christian (first wife) on March 29, 1813, and Julia Gardiner (second wife) on June 26, 1844.

Religion: Episcopalian.

Political party: Whig.

Term of office: April 6, 1841 to March 3, 1845.

Died: January 18, 1862.

Sidelight: The first president whose wife died while he was in office.

Which future president was fifty-five years old when he ran for and won his first elected public office?
Ronald Reagan was that age when he became governor of California for the first time.

How many presidents, excluding those who died in office, did not attend the inauguration of their successors?
Three:

John Adams. Not only was he deeply hurt by losing the election to Thomas Jefferson, he was grieving over the death of his son, Charles. He wanted to return home quickly.

John Quincy Adams. The campaign of 1828 was a vicious one, with much mudslinging on both sides. Adams had no love for Andrew Jackson and refused to attend.

Andrew Johnson. He hated Grant and refused to attend.

How many presidents were professional soldiers?
Four:

William Henry Harrison

Zachary Taylor

Ulysses S. Grant

Dwight David Eisenhower

How many presidents became widowers while in office?
Three wives of presidents died while their husbands were in office:

Letitia Tyler, wife of John Tyler

Caroline Harrison, wife of Benjamin Harrison

Ellen Wilson, wife of Woodrow Wilson

How many presidents served less than one term?
  Ten:

  William Henry Harrison—died in office
  John Tyler—finished Harrison's term
  Zachary Taylor—died in office
  Millard Fillmore—finished Taylor's term
  Andrew Johnson—finished Lincoln's term
  James A. Garfield—assassinated
  Chester A. Arthur—finished Garfield's term
  Warren G. Harding—died in office
  John F. Kennedy—assassinated
  Gerald R. Ford—finished Nixon's term after he
    resigned

Which presidential candidate was able to offset a political scandal and perhaps save his campaign by being a good speller?
  James A. Garfield. During the campaign of 1880, some dirty trickster forged a letter from Garfield claiming that he was in favor of the unlimited importation of Chinese laborers into the U.S. This forgery was meant to make Garfield lose thousands and thousands of votes of American workers who were afraid they would lose their jobs to immigrants.

  The letter, however, contained two spelling errors, and since Garfield was an excellent speller, the forgery was exposed, and Garfield went on to become president.

Presidents Zachary Taylor and James Madison were distant relatives. What was their relationship?
  They were second cousins.

How many presidents have been lawyers?
Twenty-four:

John Adams	Rutherford B. Hayes
Thomas Jefferson	James A. Garfield
James Monroe	Chester A. Arthur
John Quincy Adams	Grover Cleveland
Andrew Jackson	Benjamin Harrison
Martin Van Buren	William McKinley
John Tyler	William Howard Taft
James K. Polk	Woodrow Wilson
Millard Fillmore	Calvin Coolidge
Franklin Pierce	Franklin Delano Roosevelt
James Buchanan	Richard M. Nixon
Abraham Lincoln	Gerald R. Ford

Which president's wife did not attend her husband's inauguration?
Jane Pierce, the wife of Franklin, did not attend her husband's inauguration, because two months before the inauguration was to take place, the Pierces' only child, eleven-year-old Benjamin, was killed in a tragic railway accident. Mrs. Pierce collapsed in grief, and for the next two years, she refused to take part in public life. She became so secluded from political life in Washington, D.C., that some persons began referring to her as the "shadow in the White House." Mrs. Pierce, in fact, wore black every day in the White House and spent much of her time writing notes to her dead son.

Who was the first president not to seek reelection?
James Knox Polk. Polk defeated Henry Clay in the presidential election of 1844, but declined to run again. Polk, in fact, was quite glad to be relieved of the responsibilities of being president, according to a March 4, 1849 entry in his diary.

James Knox Polk

11th President

Born: November 2, 1795, in Mecklenburg County, North Carolina.

Father: Samuel Polk.

Mother: Jane Knox Polk.

Married: Sarah Childress on January 1, 1824.

Religion: Presbyterian.

Political party: Democratic.

Term of office: March 4, 1845 to March 3, 1849.

Died: June 15, 1849.

Sidelight: While Polk was president, gold was discovered in California.

Who was the last president to be born in a log cabin?
James A. Garfield, who was born November 19, 1831, in Ohio.

Which president inadvertently created one of America's most famous advertising slogans?

Theodore Roosevelt. The Maxwell House Coffee slogan— "Good to the last drop"— was actually a remark made by Theodore Roosevelt while he attended a dinner party. The Maxwell House people later adopted the president's words as their slogan.

For whom did Ronald Reagan campaign in the presidential election of 1948?
Reagan campaigned for the democratic candidate, Harry S Truman. Mr. Reagan did not become a Republican until 1952, although, as a Democrat, he supported the candidacies of both Eisenhower and Nixon.

Which president held séances in the White House?
Abraham Lincoln. He and his wife had great interest in studying psychic phenomena.

Which president did not even vote in his own election?
Zachary Taylor. In fact, because Taylor was a professional soldier, who was always moving from place to place and never established an official place of residence, he did not vote in any presidential election until he was sixty-two years old.

Zachary Taylor

12th President

Born: November 24, 1784, in Montebello, Virginia.

Father: Lieutenant Colonel Richard Taylor.

Mother: Sarah Dabney Strother Taylor.

Married: Margaret Mackall Smith on June 21, 1810.

Religion: Episcopalian.

Political party: Whig.

Term of office: March 4, 1849 to July 9, 1850.

Died: July 9, 1850.

Sidelight: His horse grazed on the White House lawn.

Which president issued the proclamation establishing June 14 as Flag Day?
Woodrow Wilson, on May 30, 1916.

Although John Quincy Adams is the only son of a president to become president himself, have sons of any other presidents also tried to be elected to the White House?
Yes. Some sons who tried to become president were:

- John Scott Harrison, son of William Henry Harrison
- John Van Buren. When he was nominated in 1848 by the Free Soil Democrats, he declined the nomination in favor of his father, Martin Van Buren.
- Robert Todd Lincoln was a serious contender for the presidential nomination (although he did not receive it) at the Republican conventions of 1884 and 1888.
- Robert Alonso Taft, son of William Howard Taft, was a serious contender for the Republican nomination at the conventions of 1940, 1948, and 1952, although he was never actually nominated. From 1939 to 1953, Robert Taft was a senator from Ohio.

The father of which president served thirteen years in the New Hampshire legislature and two terms as governor of that state?
Franklin Pierce's father, Benjamin

Which president could read the Bible in four languages—Greek, Latin, French, and English?
Thomas Jefferson, perhaps the most brilliant of the presidents.

Which president refused to accept an honorary degree from Oxford University?

Millard Fillmore. He refused the honorary degree because he felt he had "neither literary nor scientific attainment." He was most likely correct.

Millard Fillmore

13th President

Born: January 7, 1800, in Locke Township (now Summerhill), New York.

Father: Nathaniel Fillmore.

Mother: Phoebe Millard Fillmore.

Stepmother: Eunice Love.

Married: Abigail Powers (first wife) on February 5, 1826, and Caroline Carmichael McIntosh (second wife) on February 10, 1858.

Religion: Unitarian.

Political party: Whig.

Term of office: July 10, 1850 to March 3, 1853.

Died: March 8, 1874.

Sidelight: He was the first president to have a stepmother.

Why do presidents use so many different pens when they sign official documents?

The pens are handed out to friends and supporters as souvenirs. The following newspaper story gives a good example of the lengths presidents go to build up goodwill.

TEN PENS, ONE SIGNATURE

September 2, 1935. Washington, D.C. If presidential signatures on noted laws should look a little joggly to future historians, it should not be surprising. What if they had to sign their names with ten pens? That's the number President Franklin Roosevelt used on the Guffey Coal Control Bill. And some say he has used as many as thirty writing a single signature! The pens generally are given as souvenirs to congressmen.

Nathaniel Hawthorne, the author of such great books as *The Scarlet Letter* **and** *The House of the Seven Gables,* **wrote the official campaign biography of which president?**

Hawthorne wrote the biography of Franklin Pierce. The two had been classmates at Bowdoin College in Maine.

Which president, while he was in office, gambled away in a single hand of poker an entire set of White House china dating back to the administration of Benjamin Harrison?

Warren G. Harding. He played poker regularly with what he called his "poker cabinet."

**The red carnation became the
state flower of Ohio in part because
which president wore that flower
in his lapel for good luck?**

  William McKinley

**Which president was forced by his mother to wear
dresses until he was five years old?**
  Franklin Delano Roosevelt. He didn't wear long
  pants until age eight.

**How many states were in the United States when George
Washington was elected president?**
  Eleven, not thirteen as you might expect. The reason
  is that neither Rhode Island nor North Carolina had
  yet ratified the Constitution when Washington was
  elected. North Carolina ratified the Constitution six
  months later, and Rhode Island officially joined the
  Union a year later.

**Between March 4, 1861, and January 18, 1862, five
ex-presidents were still alive. Who were they?**
  Martin Van Buren, John Tyler, Millard Fillmore,
  Franklin Pierce, and James Buchanan. As of January 1, 1991, four ex-presidents are still alive: Richard
  M. Nixon, Jimmy Carter, Gerald R. Ford, and Ronald Reagan.

Which president attended Bowdoin College in Maine—where, in his sophomore year, he was such a poor student that he held the lowest grades of anyone in his class?

Franklin Pierce. After his second year in college, however, he changed his study habits. By the time he graduated from Bowdoin in 1824, he ranked third in his class. Pierce became friends at college with the future great novelist Nathaniel Hawthorne.

Franklin Pierce

14th President

Born: November 23, 1804, in Hillsborough, New Hampshire.

Father: General Benjamin Pierce.

Mother: Anna Kendrick.

Married: Jane Means Appleton on November 10, 1834.

Religion: Episcopalian.

Political party: Democratic.

Term of office: March 4, 1853 to March 3, 1857.

Died: October 8, 1869.

Sidelight: He was only forty-eight years old when elected president.

Did Abraham Lincoln have a substitute fight for him in the Civil War?

Yes, but not a paid substitute that he hired to fight in his place, as some rich men did during the Civil War.

When J. Summerfield Staples, the son of an army chaplain, heard that Lincoln felt that the president himself should be actually fighting in the war (but he could not because of all the duties of his office), Staples volunteered to be Lincoln's substitute. Mr. Staples served as a private and both he and his father survived the war and returned home to Stroudsburg, Pennsylvania.

Should you travel to the cemetery there, you can see a headstone that reads:

> *J. Summerfield Staples*
> *A private of*
> *Co. C176 Reg. P.V.*
> *Also a member of the*
> *2, Reg. D.C. Vol.*
> *A substitute for*
> *Abraham Lincoln*
> *died*
> *Jan. 11, 1888*
> *Aged 43 yrs,—4 mos. &*
> *27 days*

Who was the first woman to vote for her son in a presidential election?

Sara Delano Roosevelt, mother of Franklin. Franklin, by the way, always addressed her as "dear Mama."

Have any presidents been the sons of clergymen?
    Yes. Three so far: Chester A. Arthur, Grover Cleveland, and Woodrow Wilson.

Which president was nicknamed "Old Buck"?
    James Buchanan. "Buck" is a play upon the pronunciation of his last name.

James Buchanan

15th President

Born: April 23, 1791, in Cove Gap, Pennsylvania.

Father: James Buchanan.

Mother: Elizabeth Speer Buchanan.

Never married.

Religion: Presbyterian.

Political party: Democratic.

Term of office: March 4, 1857 to March 3, 1861.

Died: June 1, 1868.

Sidelight: The first president to be born in Pennsylvania. By the time he was thirty years old he had amassed a fortune of $300,000.

Which president had a dream that prophesied his assassination?

Abraham Lincoln. Lincoln's story of his dream is one of the strangest stories ever to come from the White House, and it was substantiated by Ward H. Lamon, Lincoln's Illinois law partner.

Because Lincoln had received numerous letters from persons threatening to kill him, he began to have troubling dreams. In one dream, which he related to his wife and Mr. Lamon, Lincoln was walking through the White House and heard many people weeping and sobbing. He entered the East Room and there he saw a coffin. In his dream, Lincoln turned to a soldier and asked, "Who is dead in the White House?" The soldier looked at Lincoln and replied, "The president. He was killed by an assassin!"

It is recorded that Lincoln had that dream again on April 14, 1865, the night before he went to Ford's Theater, where he was killed by John Wilkes Booth!

Which president was so overweight that opponents sometimes referred to him as "His Rotundity"?

John Adams

Which president died in a bed that had been previously occupied by his assassin?

Abraham Lincoln. After Lincoln was shot by John Wilkes Booth at Ford's Theater, Lincoln was quickly moved across the street to a boarding house for actors. By a strange coincidence, Lincoln was placed in the same room previously occupied by Booth.

Abraham Lincoln

16th President

Born: February 12, 1809, in Hardin County, Kentucky.

Father: Thomas Lincoln.

Mother: Nancy Hanks Lincoln.

Married: Mary Todd on November 4, 1842.

Religion: No formal affiliation.

Political party: Republican.

Term of office: March 4, 1861 to April 15, 1865.

Died: April 15, 1865.

Sidelight: Lincoln was the first president to die by assassination.

Which president was so large that when he moved into the White House, he had to have a bathtub built that was so big it could accommodate four average-sized men?
William Howard Taft. He was six feet tall and weighed over 300 pounds.

Which president weighed less than 100 pounds?
James Madison. He stood only five feet four inches (the shortest of our presidents) and was very slight of build.

Which president said that his sister had been his best friend and that "She loved me as an only sister loves a brother whom she imagines almost perfect, and I loved her as an only brother loves a sister who is perfect"?
Rutherford B. Hayes. His sister, Mrs. Fanny A. Platt, died in 1856, shortly after she delivered stillborn twins. The death of his sister was a shattering blow to the future president.

What epitaph did John Adams suggest for himself?
"Here lies John Adams who took upon himself the responsibility of peace with France in the year 1800."

Which president was both the son of a signer of the Declaration of Independence and the grandfather of a president?
William Henry Harrison, grandfather to President Benjamin Harrison.

The popular song "Listen to the Mockingbird" was dedicated to the niece of which president?
"Listen to the Mockingbird" was dedicated to Harriet Lane, niece of James Buchanan. Since President Buchanan was a bachelor, Miss Lane acted as the official White House hostess during her uncle's presidency.

Which president kept a pet mockingbird in his White House study?
Thomas Jefferson, who was so fond of his pet that he taught the bird to take food from between his lips.

Was the city of Lincoln, Illinois, named in honor of Abraham Lincoln before or after he became president?
Strangely enough, Lincoln, Illinois, was named to honor Lincoln even before he became our sixteenth president. Lincoln, in fact, helped to plan the city, and on August 22, 1853, he christened the town by hurling a watermelon over a stack of timber. At the time Lincoln was a successful lawyer in Logan County.

What is the wording of the oath of office that each president takes?
The oath of office, as prescribed by article II, section 1 of the Constitution, reads:

I do solemnly swear (or affirm) that I will faithfully execute the office of president of the United States, and will to the best of my ability, preserve, protect and defend the constitution of the United States.

Which president's wife is frequently credited with having the U.S. Marine Band play "Hail to the Chief" whenever the president appeared on occasions of state?

John Tyler's second wife, Julia.

Which president never went to school?

Andrew Johnson. He was taught to read and to write by his wife.

Andrew Johnson

17th President

Born: December 29, 1808, in Raleigh, North Carolina.

Father: Jacob Johnson.

Mother: Mary McDonough Johnson.

Married: Eliza McCardle on May 5, 1827.

Religion: No formal affiliation.

Political party: Democratic.

Term of office: April 15, 1865 to March 3, 1869.

Died: July 31, 1875.

Sidelight: During Andrew Johnson's term the thirteenth Amendment to the Constitution—the amendment that officially abolished slavery—was ratified.

Which former president, after the death of his first wife, married his wife's niece?
    Benjamin Harrison. His second marriage so angered his children that they refused to attend the wedding ceremony.

Which twentieth century president refused to use the telephone while he was in office?
    Calvin Coolidge. Just another reason to call him Silent Cal.

What future president became a college president at twenty-six?
    James A. Garfield. He graduated from Williams College, and in 1857 he became president of Hiram College (formerly the Western Reserve Eclectic Institute). The college at that time had only five faculty members.

How many presidents have been only children?
    None. All of our presidents have had either brothers or sisters.

Which president smoked twenty cigars every day of his adult life?
    Ulysses S. Grant

Ulysses Simpson Grant

18th President

Born: April 27, 1822, in Point Pleasant, Ohio.

Father: Jesse Root Grant.

Mother: Hannah Simpson Grant.

Married: Julia Boggs Dent on August 22, 1848.

Religion: Methodist.

Political party: Republican.

Term of office: March 4, 1869 to March 3, 1877.

Died: July 23, 1885.

Sidelight: During Grant's presidency, the telephone was invented by Alexander Graham Bell.

Which president once issued an order that forbade swearing throughout the U.S. army?

George Washington issued such an order, even though his own vocabulary often left much to be desired.

Which president was so fond of the works of Edgar Allan Poe that he made it a practice to read some of Poe's stories at least once a year?

Abraham Lincoln. According to the noted editor and novelist William Dean Howells, the heart of Lincoln's mind "is mathematical and metaphysical and he is therefore pleased with the absolute and logical method of Poe's tales and sketches in which the problem of mystery is given, and wrought out into everyday facts by the process of cunning analysis. It is said that he suffers no year to pass without a perusal of this author."

Which president never knew his father, because his father had contracted a fever and had died eleven weeks before the son was born?

Rutherford B. Hayes. Hayes was named in honor of his father who died in 1822.

Rutherford Birchard Hayes

19th President

Born: October 4, 1822, in Delaware, Ohio.

Father: Rutherford Hayes.

Mother: Sophia Birchard Hayes.

Married: Lucy Ware Webb on December 30, 1852.

Religion: No formal affiliation.

Political party: Republican.

Term of office: March 4, 1877 to March 3, 1881.

Died: January 17, 1893.

Sidelight: Hayes was the first president to visit the West Coast while in office. He arrived in San Francisco on September 8, 1880. (Trick question for your friends: What U.S. president was born in both Delaware and Ohio?)

Which president was such an avid reader that he frequently read two or three books a day, even while he was president?

Theodore Roosevelt. Not only was he a great reader, but also he wrote quite a few books. Among books written by America's twenty-sixth president are: *Hunting Trip of a Ranchman* (1885), *Thomas Hart Benton* (1887), *History of New York City* (1891), and *The Wilderness Hunter* (1893).

Who was the first president to be born west of the Mississippi River?

Herbert Hoover, born in West Branch, Iowa, on August 10, 1874.

Who is the only president to be buried in Washington, D.C.?

Woodrow Wilson. He was buried in Washington Cathedral.

Which president described himself as "an idealist without illusions"?
John F. Kennedy

When James A. Garfield was nominated for president at the Republican convention of 1880, how many votes did he receive on the first ballot?
None.

James Abram Garfield

20th President

Born: November 19, 1831, in Orange, Ohio.

Father: Abram Garfield.

Mother: Eliza Ballou Garfield.

Married: Lucretia Rudolph on November 11, 1858.

Religion: Disciples of Christ.

Political party: Republican.

Term of office: March 4, 1881 to September 19, 1881.

Died: September 19, 1881.

Sidelight: He was our first left-handed president.

When President Garfield was assassinated, what world-famous inventor was called to the president's hospital room to help locate the bullet in his body?

Alexander Graham Bell, the inventor of the telephone, was brought in to assist Garfield's doctors, who were unable to find the bullet in the president's wound. Bell had constructed an electronic listening device, but it was all to no avail. The bullet could not be found.

Indeed, the constant probing of the wound brought about severe infection which eventually caused Garfield's death.

The last name of which president means "son of God's place"?

Jefferson. According to an article in the December 6, 1890, issue of *American Notes and Queries,* a reader reported that Jefferson "is a Welsh name. He says in his autobiography that his ancestors came to this country from Wales and from near Mount Snowden. It means the son of Jeffer, which is a corruption of the name Geoffrey, which means 'God's Place.' "

Which president wrote to his young daughter to advise her never to go out in the sun without a bonnet "because it will make you very ugly and then we should not love you so much"?

Thomas Jefferson, to his daughter Mary.

In 1932, Sigmund Freud co-authored a psychological biography of which president?

Woodrow Wilson, although the book was not published until 1967.

Which president demanded—before he would move into the White House—that all the old White House furniture be auctioned off?

Chester A. Arthur. He then refurnished the White House in the Victorian style.

Chester Alan Arthur

21st President

Born: October 5, 1830, in Fairfield, Vermont.

Father: William Arthur.

Mother: Malvina Stone Arthur.

Married: Ellen Lewis Herndon on October 25, 1859.

Religion: Episcopalian.

Political party: Republican.

Term of office: September 19, 1881 to March 3, 1885.

Died: November 18, 1886.

Sidelight: Arthur's wife died before he became president and so Arthur's sister, Mary Arthur McElroy, assumed the official duties of White House hostess.

Has any president been born on July 4?
Yes. Just one, Calvin Coolidge, who was born on July 4, 1872.

How many presidents have died on the Fourth of July?
Three. John Adams, Thomas Jefferson, and James Monroe, who died in 1831.

Which president, upon his death bed, uttered as his dying words, "Thomas Jefferson survives"?
John Adams. Adams unfortunately was wrong. Jefferson had died a few hours earlier. Both men died on July 4, 1826.

Which president wrote the following love poem when he was in his teens?

Ah! woe's me, that I should love and conceal,
Long have I wish'd but never dare reveal
Even though severely Love's pain I feel.

George Washington

Which president said, "No man should be allowed to be president who doesn't understand hogs"?
Harry S Truman

Which president regularly swam nude in the Potomac River at 5 A.M.?

John Quincy Adams. His nude swimming (bathing suits had not been invented in Adams's day) brought about the first presidential interview with a woman reporter, Anne Royall, who was America's first female professional journalist. She had been refused interviews with the president, but she was aware of the president's daily schedule. When she saw Adams swimming in the Potomac, she gathered up all his clothing and sat on it. She refused to leave until President Adams granted her the interview.

Which vice president (who later became president) was drunk when he took his oath of office?

Andrew Johnson, in 1865. His drunkenness, however, was excusable. He had been taking large amounts of alcohol to ease the pain brought on by a bout with typhoid fever.

Which president had an artificial jaw of vulcanized rubber?

Grover Cleveland. During his presidential term, doctors discovered that Cleveland was suffering from cancer of the mouth. Most of Cleveland's left jaw had to be removed and he was then fitted with an artificial jaw made of rubber.

Grover Cleveland

22nd & 24th President

Born: March 18, 1837, in Caldwell, New Jersey.

Father: Richard Falley Cleveland.

Mother: Anne Neal Cleveland.

Married: Frances Folsom on June 2, 1886.

Religion: Presbyterian.

Political party: Democratic.

Terms of office: March 4, 1885 to March 3, 1889 and March 4, 1893 to March 3, 1897.

Died: June 24, 1908.

Sidelight: Cleveland, our twenty-second and twenty-fourth president, is the only president to have served two nonconsecutive terms.

What was the "Petticoat Government"?

"Petticoat Government" refers to the time when President Woodrow Wilson was incapacitated by a severe stroke and the government was, in effect, run by Wilson's wife, Edith. Edith did everything in her power to keep the public unaware of the severity of her husband's condition.

How many presidents were born in log cabins?
Four:

Millard Fillmore

James Buchanan

Abraham Lincoln

James A. Garfield

What future president, while attending Amherst College, received only one vote when his classmates voted which student would be "Most Likely to Succeed"?
Calvin Coolidge. The classmate the Amherst seniors selected as the one most likely to succeed was Dwight Morrow, who later became ambassador to Mexico.

Who was the first president of all fifty states?
On January 3, 1959 Alaska was proclaimed the forty-ninth state. Hawaii became a state on March 18, 1959. Dwight David Eisenhower was the president at the time.

Who was the first president to have a Christmas tree in the White House?
Benjamin Harrison

Benjamin Harrison

23rd President

Born: August 20, 1833, in North Bend, Ohio.

Father: John Scott Harrison.

Mother: Elizabeth Ramsey Irwin Harrison.

Married: Caroline Lavinia Scott (first wife) on October 20, 1853, and Mary Scott Lord Dimmick (second wife) on April 6, 1896.

Religion: Presbyterian.

Political party: Republican.

Term of office: March 4, 1889 to March 3, 1893.

Died: March 13, 1901.

Sidelight: He grew up in a family of thirteen children. He was the second president whose wife died while he was in office.

The faces of which four presidents are carved upon Mount Rushmore?

Washington, Lincoln, Jefferson, and Theodore Roosevelt. Alfred Hitchcock's great suspense film *North by Northwest,* which features a scene on Mount Rushmore, was originally titled *The Man on Lincoln's Nose.*

The fiancée of which future president commited suicide?
Ann Caroline Coleman, the fiancée of James Buchanan. She was the daughter of a wealthy ironmaster, and her family strongly disapproved of Buchanan. At age twenty-eight, she committed suicide after a lovers' quarrel. The family (although they themselves might well have been the cause) blamed Buchanan for the death of their daughter. Buchanan was heartbroken and never married.

Which president was so tone deaf that he could not recognize the national anthem when it was played?
William Howard Taft. Whenever the national anthem was played, Taft had to be nudged by his secretary so that he would know when to stand up.

Which president kept a pet parrot in the White House that could whistle "Yankee Doodle"?

William McKinley. He would whistle the first part of "Yankee Doodle" and the parrot would complete the tune.

William McKinley

25th President

Born: January 29, 1843, in Niles, Ohio.
Father: William McKinley.
Mother: Nancy Campbell Allison McKinley.
Married: Ida Saxton on January 25, 1871.
Religion: Methodist.
Political party: Republican.
Term of office: March 4, 1897 to September 14, 1901.
Died: September 14, 1901.
Sidelight: McKinley's wife, Ida, was an epileptic and suffered a seizure during the second inaugural ball.

Which president said: "I have come to the conclusion that the major part of the president is to increase the gate receipts of expositions and fairs and bring tourists to town."
William Howard Taft

Which president, after leaving office, ran in 1856 as the unsuccessful candidate of the American, or Know-Nothing, party?

Millard Fillmore. The American, or Know-Nothing, party was formed, in part, to counter the consequences of the large numbers of immigrants coming into the United States. Members of the party feared the loss of jobs to foreigners, but when questioned about the party's activities, they claimed to "know nothing." Hence, the party's name.

The Know-Nothing party wanted only American-born Protestants elected to public office, and in 1856 they nominated Millard Fillmore as their presidential candidate. Fillmore managed to carry only one state—Maryland.

George Washington was frequently referred to as being "First in war, first in peace, first in the hearts of his countrymen." What is the origin of that description?

On December 26, 1799, General Henry Lee (father of Robert E. Lee) delivered a funeral oration for George Washington before both houses of Congress. He used that phrase which has since become one of the best known descriptions of America's first president.

How many copies of Lincoln's Gettysburg Address in his own handwriting are still in existence?

Five copies, thus disproving the legend that Lincoln composed his great speech on the back of an envelope while he was traveling on the train from Washington. One copy of the speech, spoken by President Lincoln at the dedication of the Soldiers' National Cemetery at Gettysburg, Pennsylvania, on November 19, 1863, hangs in the Lincoln Room of the White House. It reads:

Four score and seven years ago our fathers brought forth on this continent, a new nation, conceived in Liberty, and dedicated to the proposition that all men are created equal.

Now we are engaged in a great civil war, testing whether that nation, or any nation so conceived and so dedicated, can long endure. We are met on a great battle-field of that war. We have come to dedicate a portion of that field, as a final resting place for those who here gave their lives that that nation might live. It is altogether fitting and proper that we should do this.

But, in a larger sense, we can not dedicate— we can not consecrate—we can not hallow— this ground. The brave men, living and dead, who struggled here, have consecrated it, far above our poor power to add or detract. The world will little note, nor long remember what we say here, but it can never forget what they did here. It is for us the living, rather, to be dedicated here to the unfinished work which they who fought here have thus far so nobly advanced. It is rather for us to be here dedicated to the great task remaining before us— that from these honored dead we take increased devotion to that cause for which they gave the last full measure of devotion—that we here highly resolve that these dead shall not have died in vain—that this nation, under God, shall have a new birth of freedom—and that government of the people, by the people, for the people, shall not perish from the earth.

Which president was once described as "one of the most mediocre-looking men ever to run for president"?
Rutherford B. Hayes, who was five feet eight inches tall, with blue eyes and red hair. He was not all that handsome, however, and so his appearance didn't appeal to some persons.

Who was the only president to write a book of poetry?
John Quincy Adams, who produced a 108-page book of poems in 1832. The book was titled *Poems of Religion and Society*. A friend had informed Adams that several young ladies in his district had requested Adams's autograph for them. To grant his friend a favor, Adams wrote stanzas to his poem— "The Wants of Man"—on separate sheets of notepaper. The opening stanza of that twenty-five stanza poem reads:

> *"Man wants but little here below,*
>   *Nor wants that little long."*
> *'Tis not with me exactly so.*
>   *But 'tis so in the song.*
> *My wants are many, and if told*
>   *Would muster many a score,*
> *And were each with a mint of gold,*
>   *I still should long for more.*

Among the other poems in the president's collection are "Hymn for the Twenty-Second of December," "Written in Sickness," "To a Bereaved Mother," and "The Hour Glass."

72

Who was the first president to support the drafting of young men into the army?

George Washington. On May 8, 1792, Congress, under Washington's administration, passed the National Conscription Act, which required "each and every free able-bodied white male citizen of the republic to serve in the U.S. Militia."

The wife of which president was the first White House hostess to hold a formal press conference?

After her husband took office Eleanor Roosevelt used to invite members of the press to meet with her on Mondays. Mrs. Roosevelt wanted to give women reporters, who were not allowed to attend the official presidential press conferences, access to information.

Which president named his home "Peaceful"?

John Adams. At age fifty-seven, Adams paid £600—a goodly sum in those days—for the house and property (some eighty-three acres of land in Quincy, Massachusetts), and gave it the name "Peaceful" because he hoped, after years of strenuous public service, that he would find tranquility there.

Who was the first president to throw out the opening ball for the major league baseball season?

William Howard Taft started the tradition of the president opening the baseball season by tossing out the first ball. In 1910, President Taft attended the opening day contest between the Washington Senators and the Philadelphia Athletics. Walter Johnson pitched a one-hitter and the Senators beat the Athletics three to nothing.

Which president kept a cow on the White House lawn so that he could have fresh milk?
William Howard Taft, but it is such a good idea, other presidents might also have done it.

George Washington initiated the custom of holding a presidential reception in the White House on New Year's Day. That custom remained in practice until January 1, 1934. Why was the custom abandoned?
The custom came to an end when Franklin Delano Roosevelt became president. Roosevelt, because he suffered from infantile paralysis, found it too difficult to stand in a receiving line.

Who was the youngest person to be elected president?
John Fitzgerald Kennedy was forty-three years old when he was elected president in 1960.

Kennedy was our youngest *elected* president, but he was not our youngest president. That honor goes to Theodore Roosevelt, who was forty-two years old when he assumed office after the assassination of McKinley.

Which president said of himself, "No president has ever enjoyed himself as much as I"?

Theodore Roosevelt, who was always known for his great zest and enthusiasm.

Theodore Roosevelt

26th President

Born: October 27, 1858, in New York, New York.

Father: Theodore Roosevelt.

Mother: Martha Bulloch Roosevelt.

Married: Alice Hathaway Lee (first wife) on October 27, 1880, and Edith Kermit Carow (second wife) on December 2, 1886.

Religion: Dutch Reformed.

Political party: Republican.

Term of office: September 14, 1901 to March 3, 1909.

Died: January 6, 1919.

Sidelight: As a child, Teddy Roosevelt suffered asthma attacks and was too sickly to attend school.

What is *The President's Mystery Plot?*

The President's Mystery Plot is a mystery (originally published as a serial in *Liberty* magazine and in book form by Farrar and Rinehart) which was based upon a plot idea by Franklin Delano Roosevelt.

According to the introduction by Arthur S. Schlesinger, Jr., in a republication of the book by Prentice-Hall, Inc., the idea for the book came about one evening in 1935, when the president was entertaining a few friends at an informal supper. President Roosevelt asked, "How can a man disappear with five million dollars in any negotiable form and not be traced?"

Among the authors who took up the challenge and contributed chapters to the mystery were Rupert Hughes, Samuel Hopkin Adams, Anthony Abbot, Rita Weiman, S. S. Van Dine, and John Erskine.

According to Mr. Schlesinger, "There is no record of Roosevelt's reaction to what *Liberty* did with his plot. Presidents relax in a variety of ways, and floating the anecdote probably satisfied FDR's sense of fun. He did receive $9,000 from *Liberty* and $72.27 from Farrar and Rinehart (which published the serial in book form), all of which went to the Warm Springs Foundation."

Which president was one of the world's more serious stamp collectors?

Franklin Delano Roosevelt, who amassed a collection of some 25,000 stamps, kept in forty albums. While he was president, he frequently suggested designs for stamps. At his death, his collection was worth millions of dollars.

Who were America's best baseball-playing presidents?
Probably William Howard Taft, who, in spite of his size, was a good second baseman (he could also hit the ball with power) and George Bush, who played for Yale's baseball team.

William Howard Taft

27th President

Born: September 15, 1857, in Cincinnati, Ohio.

Father: Alphonso Taft.

Mother: Louisa Maria Torrey Taft.

Married: Helen Herron on June 19, 1886.

Religion: Unitarian.

Political party: Republican.

Term of office: March 4, 1909 to March 3, 1913.

Died: March 8, 1930.

Sidelight: It was during Taft's term as president that the Sixteenth Amendment to the Constitution was ratified, the amendment that established federal income tax.

Which future president, after he failed to receive the Democratic nomination for governor of his state, turned to religion and became a born-again Christian?

Jimmy Carter. In 1966, he was not nominated for governor of Georgia and that became the first serious political setback of his career. In 1970, he once again sought the nomination for governor and succeeded.

What president avoided all allusions to the Bible in private letters and public utterances?

James Madison. Although he was an Episcopalian, he was not a very devout one.

Which president, after leaving office, became the chancellor of the University of Buffalo?

Millard Fillmore

Which president, upon leaving the White House, said, "I am glad to be going. This is the lonesomest place in the world"?

William Howard Taft. Unlike Teddy Roosevelt, Taft did not enjoy being president. Indeed, he had his heart set upon becoming a Supreme Court justice, an ambition he finally achieved in 1921.

Who was the first president to be photographed?
John Quincy Adams

How many presidents did not go to college?
Nine. Harry S Truman, Grover Cleveland, Andrew Johnson, Abraham Lincoln, Millard Fillmore, Zachary Taylor, Martin Van Buren, Andrew Jackson, and George Washington.

Which president, while still in office, actually led a military force to put down a rebellion?
George Washington. In July 1794, farmers in western Pennsylvania refused to support a federal excise tax on liquor and went into open rebellion. The following month, President Washington issued a proclamation ordering the rebels to return home. At the same time the militia from four states was called up. On September 24 Washington issued a proclamation ordering the militia to supress the Whisky Rebellion. For a short time, George Washington himself marched at the head of the force.

Which president, before Super Bowl VI, called Don Shula, the coach of the Miami Dolphins, to recommend a play?

Richard M. Nixon. Unfortunately, the play he recommended didn't work.

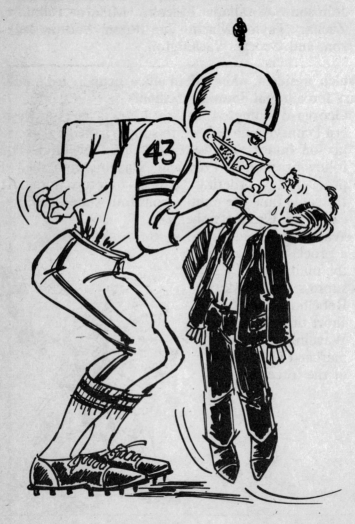

Which future president was such a slow learner that he was unable to read until he was nine years old?

Woodrow Wilson. Amazingly, that slow-to-learn reader went on to earn a doctoral degree from Johns Hopkins University in 1886. Wilson's doctoral dissertation was called *Congressional Government, a Study in American Politics.* So far Wilson is the only president to earn a Ph.D.

Woodrow Wilson

28th President

Born: December 28, 1856, in Staunton, Virginia.

Father: Joseph Ruggles Wilson.

Mother: Jessie Janet Woodrow Wilson.

Married: Ellen Louise Axson (first wife) on June 24, 1885, and Edith Bolling Galt (second wife) on December 18, 1915.

Religion: Presbyterian.

Political party: Democratic.

Term of office: March 4, 1913 to March 3, 1921.

Died: February 3, 1924.

Sidelight: He was only the second Democrat since the Civil War to be elected president.

What does the campaign cry "Buck and Breck" refer to?
During the presidential campaign of 1856, "Buck and Breck" was a shorthand way of referring to the Democratic candidates for president and vice president, James Buchanan and John C. Breckinridge. When Buchanan won the election, Breckinridge became, at age thirty-six, the youngest man to become vice president.

Which future president, while he was secretary of state, tried to negotiate the sale of Cuba to the United States?
James Buchanan, while he was secretary of state under Polk. During Polk's administration the U.S. attempted to purchase Cuba from Spain for $120,000,000.

Which president's son was on hand at the assassination of three presidents?
Robert Todd Lincoln, son of Abraham Lincoln, who was on hand or nearby at the assassinations of Lincoln, Garfield, and McKinley. He considered himself a jinx and decided never to attend any presidential functions.

In 1855, a black woman was, because of her color, ejected from a Brooklyn streetcar. What future president represented her case and won $500 for her?
Chester A. Arthur. Not only did he win the case for his client, but also the case brought about better treatment for all blacks on New York's public transportation system.

How many of the fifty states are named after presidents?
Only the state of Washington, named in honor of George Washington.

Which future president was the first member of Congress to go on active duty in World War II?

Lyndon B. Johnson, who was commissioned as a lieutenant commander with the naval reserves in 1940. Shortly after the Japanese attack on Pearl Harbor, he went on active duty. Johnson was brave in battle and received the Silver Star for gallantry in action when the patrol bomber he was flying was fired upon by Japanese Zeros near Port Moresby, New Guinea.

Which future president once wrote a film treatment of the life of John Paul Jones and tried to sell it to the Famous Players–Lasky Corporation?

Franklin Delano Roosevelt wrote a twenty-nine page film treatment on John Paul Jones in 1923. The introductory remarks to the treatment state that "In the following episodes, based on the latest historical research, the correct chronology has been faithfully followed. I have selected the principal incidents which formed his character and led to the making of one of the sincerest patriots of the American struggle for independence, and the greatest naval hero of the American people."

After receiving a letter from Adolph Zukor's assistant (Eugene J. Zukor) on May 2, 1923, Mr. Roosevelt sent off his treatment to the Famous Players–Lasky Corporation (now Paramount Pictures), but, like any other screenwriter, he was left without a response to his material for over a year. Finally, on July 22, 1924, Roosevelt wrote to Mr. Zukor and asked for the return of his treatment.

A film from the material was never made.

Who was the Republican party's first presidential candidate?
John G. Fremont, who ran in 1856. Tremont was defeated by James Buchanan.

Which president once worked as a clerk in a post office?
William McKinley. And here is a McKinley joke you can try on your friends—ask them which president was raised in Poland. When they give up, tell them that the answer is McKinley. He was raised in the town of Poland, Ohio.

Which president sometimes took his White House guests on strolls through the streets of Washington, D.C., as late as three or four o'clock in the morning?
President Chester A. Arthur loved to stay up late. He rarely went to bed before 2 A.M.

Who was the first president to ride in an automobile to his inauguration?
Warren G. Harding on March 4, 1921.

Warren Gamaliel Harding

29th President

Born: November 2, 1865, near Corsica (now Blooming Grove), Ohio.

Father: George Tyron Harding.

Mother: Phoebe Elizabeth Dickerson Harding.

Married: Florence Kling De Wolfe on July 8, 1891.

Religion: Baptist.

Political party: Republican.

Term of office: March 4, 1921 to August 2, 1923.

Died: August 2, 1923.

Sidelight: He was the first newspaper publisher to be elected president. He wrote two books: *Rededicating America* (1920) and *Our Common Country* (1921).

**The title of Ronald Reagan's autobiography is called
Where's the Rest of Me? Why did he choose such a
strange title?**

The title comes from a line in the 1941 movie *King's
Row*. In that film Ronald Reagan portrays a small-
town playboy named Drake McHugh, whose legs
are needlessly amputated by a vengeful surgeon.
After the operation, when the character wakes up,
he asks: "Where's the rest of me?"

What does the initial *S* stand for in Harry S Truman?

The *S* does not stand for any name at all (hence it is
frequently written without a period following the
letter). Truman's parents could not agree on either
Shipper, in honor of his paternal grandfather, or
Solomon, in honor of his mother's father. The S,
therefore, was a compromise.

**Which president's mother was such a Southerner that,
when she visited her son in the White House, she refused
to occupy the Lincoln guest room?**

Martha Ellen Young (1852–1947), Harry S Truman's mother, grew up in a pro-Confederate household during the Civil War, and her family for a time
was forced out of their home by Union soldiers.
When Truman became president, Martha bragged
to reporters that she was no Yankee and refused to
sleep in the bed once occupied by Abraham Lincoln
when she visited the White House.

**Which president claimed that by the time he was fifteen,
he had read every book in his local library?**

Harry S Truman of Independence, Missouri. He was
a shy boy who made, according to his own description, "books his sport."

Which president served longer than any other president?
Franklin Delano Roosevelt, who held office from 1933 until his death in 1945. He was the only president elected to four terms.

How was Franklin Delano Roosevelt related to Theodore Roosevelt?
Teddy Roosevelt was Franklin's fifth cousin. Teddy was also Eleanor Roosevelt's uncle and he was the one who gave her in marriage to Franklin.

When this young boy was taken to the White House to meet President Grover Cleveland, Cleveland told the boy he hoped the boy would never have the misfortune of becoming president of the United States. Ironically, the young boy did grow up to become president. Who was he?
Franklin Delano Roosevelt

Who was the first president to wear contact lenses?
Ronald Reagan

The first American ever to receive a Nobel Prize was a president. Who was he?

Theodore Roosevelt. Because of his role in bringing about a settlement to the Russo-Japanese War (1904–1905) President Roosevelt was voted the Nobel Peace Prize. He received it in 1906.

The father of which president had nine children and gave each of them a million dollars when he or she turned twenty-one?

John F. Kennedy's father, Joseph P. Kennedy

Which president once said, "If you don't say anything, you won't be called on to repeat it?"

Calvin Coolidge. Because he was a man of few words, he was frequently referred to as "Silent Cal." Indeed, he was so silent that when someone told the writer Dorothy Parker that President Coolidge had died, she quipped, "How can they tell?"

Calvin Coolidge

30th President

Born: July 4, 1872, in Plymouth, Vermont.

Father: John Calvin Coolidge.

Mother: Victoria Josephine Moor Coolidge.

Married: Grace Anna Goodhue on October 4, 1905.

Religion: Congregationalist.

Political party: Republican.

Term of office: August 3, 1923 to March 3, 1929.

Died: January 5, 1933.

Sidelight: In 1927, during Coolidge's presidency, Charles Lindbergh completed the first transatlantic solo flight.

What provision is there in the Constitution for notifying the winning presidential candidate of his election?

None. One can only wonder what would happen if a candidate were elected president and nobody told him or her. The winning candidate is given his first official notification when he enters (with his vice president elect) the Senate Chamber right before he takes the official oath of office.

Have any presidents ever been arrested while they held office?

Yes. At least two presidents have: Ulysses S. Grant was arrested for riding his horse too fast through Washington and was fined twenty dollars; and Franklin Pierce was arrested and charged with running over an elderly lady with his horse, but those charges were eventually dropped.

What president and his wife, when they didn't want their guests or White House staff members to know what they were saying, sometimes carried on conversations in Chinese?

Herbert Hoover and his wife, Lou

Herbert Clark Hoover

31st President

Born: August 10, 1874, in West Branch, Iowa.

Father: Jesse Clark Hoover.

Mother: Hulda Randall Minthorn Hoover.

Married: Lou Henry on February 10, 1899.

Religion: Society of Friends (Quaker).

Political party: Republican.

Term of office: March 4, 1929 to March 3, 1933.

Died: October 20, 1964.

Sidelight: As part of a survey conducted by the School of Engineering and Applied Science of Columbia University in 1964, Herbert Hoover and Thomas Edison were named the two greatest engineers in U.S. history.

Which president delivered the shortest inaugural address?

George Washington's address at his second inauguration (March 4, 1793) was only 135 words:

Fellow Citizens:

I am again called upon by the voice of my country to execute the functions of its Chief Magistrate. When the occasion proper for it shall arrive, I shall endeavor to express the high sense I entertain of this distinguished honor, and of the confidence which has been reposed in me by the people of united America.

Previous to the execution of any official act of the President the Constitution requires an oath of office. This oath I am now about to take, and in your presence: That if it shall be found during my administration of the Government I have in any instance violated willingly or knowingly the injunctions thereof, I may (besides incurring constitutional punishment) be subject to the upbraidings of all who are now witnesses of the present solemn ceremony.

Who was the first person to serve as an official speechwriter to a president?

Judson Welliver, a newspaper reporter who was hired as a speechwriter by Warren G. Harding.

Who was the first president to appear on television?

Franklin Delano Roosevelt. At the opening ceremonies for the New York World's Fair, on April 30, 1939, Roosevelt spoke into a television camera overlooking the Court of Peace. This first telecast of a United States president was produced by the National Broadcasting Company. At the time, however, there were not too many people with television sets to receive the presidential message.

Franklin Delano Roosevelt

32nd President

Born: January 30, 1882, in Hyde Park, New York.

Father: James Roosevelt.

Mother: Sara Delano Roosevelt.

Married: Anna Eleanor Roosevelt on March 17, 1905.

Religion: Episcopalian.

Political party: Democratic.

Term of office: March 4, 1933 to April 12, 1945.

Died: April 12, 1945.

Sidelight: FDR (who was nominated in 1920 to be James M. Cox's vice president) was the first defeated vice-presidential nominee to be elected president.

Which future president was a Revolutionary War soldier at age thirteen?

Andrew Jackson, who at thirteen, joined the South Carolina militia. He was taken prisoner and, when a British officer ordered Jackson to clean his boots, Jackson refused to do so. The officer then drew his sword and slashed Jackson across the forehead. The cut left an ugly scar which Jackson bore for the rest of his life.

Why was Lyndon Johnson sometimes called "Landslide Lyndon"?

In 1948, Johnson won election to the Senate by a margin of merely eighty-seven votes. The election was so close that the nickname "Landslide Lyndon" was humorously and ironically applied to him. In spite of his narrow victory, Johnson managed to remain in the Senate until 1961, when he became vice president under John F. Kennedy.

Who wrote the melodrama *The Dark Tower*, and what importance did that play have for Richard M. Nixon?

The Dark Tower was written by Alexander Woollcott and George S. Kaufman. The play, produced by Sam Harris, opened in New York in November, 1933. Margaret Hamilton, who later achieved fame by portraying the Wicked Witch of the West in the film version of *The Wizard of Oz,* was one of the members of the cast.

The play holds particular importance to former president Richard M. Nixon because it was in an amateur production of that play in Whittier, California, that he met his wife, Pat. Mr. Nixon, in his autobiography, tells about attending the tryouts for the play:

I thought I knew everyone in Whittier, but that night a beautiful and vivacious young woman with titian hair appeared whom I had never seen before. I found I could not take my eyes away from her. This new girl in town was Pat Ryan, and she had just begun teaching at Whittier High School. For me it was a case of love at first sight.

I got a friend to introduce us and then offered them both a ride home. On the way I asked Pat if she would like a date with me. She said, "I'm very busy." I said, "You shouldn't say that, because someday I am going to marry you!" We all laughed because it seemed so unlikely at the time. But I wonder whether it was a sixth sense that prompted me to make such an impetuous statement.

Mr. Nixon had previously trod the boards as the prosecuting attorney in a production of Ayn Rand's courtroom drama, *The Night of January 16th.*

Can a person be president for more than two terms?
No. In 1951, the Constitution was amended, stating that no president can serve for more than two terms.

What qualifications does a person have to meet in order to be eligible to run for president?
According to the Constitution, the president must be:

A natural born citizen

At least thirty-five years old

Fourteen years a resident of the United States

Which president could simultaneously write a sentence in Greek with his right hand and a sentence in Latin with his left?
James A. Garfield, who often performed the feat to amuse members of his cabinet.

Which future president was, as a young man, informally engaged to the daughter of a Ku Klux Klan leader?
Lyndon B. Johnson, when he was in college. Johnson's father, however, was a vehement critic of the Klan, and Johnson finally called the engagement off. Johnson later went on to play a most important part in the development of Civil Rights legislation.

How old was Thomas Jefferson when he drafted the Declaration of Independence?
Jefferson was thirty-five when he penned that famous and important document.

Who was the first president to take office during wartime?

Harry S Truman

Harry S Truman

33rd President

Born: May 8, 1884, in Lamar, Missouri.

Father: John Anderson Truman.

Mother: Martha Ellen Young Truman.

Married: Elizabeth "Bess" Virginia Wallace on June 28, 1919.

Religion: Baptist.

Political party: Democratic.

Term of office: April 12, 1945 to January 20, 1953.

Died: December 26, 1972.

Sidelight: In 1951, during Truman's presidency, the twenty-second Amendment to the Constitution was ratified. It stated: "No person shall be elected to the office of the President more than twice. . . ."

Who was the first president to be born outside the original thirteen colonies?

Our sixteenth president, Abraham Lincoln. He was born near Hodgenville, Kentucky, on February 12, 1809.

Which presidents had no children?

George and Martha Washington (but he adopted the two children from Martha's first marriage)

James and Dolley Madison

Andrew Jackson and his wife, Rachel (adopted a son)

James and Sarah Polk

James Buchanan was a bachelor

Warren G. Harding and his wife, Florence (Harding fathered an illegitimate child).

Has the wife of any president ever been accused of being a spy?

Not officially, but during the Civil War, Mary Todd Lincoln, wife of Abraham Lincoln, because her four brothers were fighting for the South, was rumored to be a Confederate spy.

How many presidents have been assassinated?

Four:

President	Date of Assassination	Assassin
Abraham Lincoln	April 14, 1865	John Wilkes Booth
James A. Garfield	July 2, 1881	Charles Guiteau
William McKinley	September 6, 1901	Leon Czolgosz
John F. Kennedy	November 22, 1963	Lee Harvey Oswald

Which presidents lived to be at least ninety years old?
As of this writing, only John Adams and Herbert Hoover. Both men died at age ninety.

When Dwight David Eisenhower was graduated from West Point what was his class rank?
Sixty-fifth in a class of 165.

Dwight David Eisenhower

34th President

Born: October 14, 1890, in Denison, Texas.

Father: David Jacob Eisenhower.

Mother: Ida Elizabeth Stover Eisenhower.

Married: Mamie Geneva Doud on July 1, 1916.

Religion: Presbyterian.

Political party: Republican.

Term of office: January 20, 1953 to January 20, 1961.

Died: March 28, 1969.

Sidelight: When he was born, Eisenhower's given name was David Dwight Eisenhower. He later switched his first two names.

When George Washington was president what was the population of the United States?
The population, as recorded by the first U.S. census in 1790, was 3,929,214. Today, the U.S. population exceeds 250,000,000.

Which president was shot by John W. Hinckley, Jr.?
Ronald Reagan, who was shot on March 30, 1981. Only quick and expert medical attention managed to save the president's life.

Which future president was once a baseball announcer, covering the Chicago Cubs games for radio?
Ronald Reagan, who broadcast games for radio station WHO in Des Moines.

Who was the first president to be born in the twentieth century?

John F. Kennedy, born on May 29, 1917.

John Fitzgerald Kennedy

35th President

Born: May 29, 1917, in Brookline, Massachusetts.

Father: Joseph Patrick Kennedy.

Mother: Rose Elizabeth Fitzgerald Kennedy.

Married: Jacqueline Lee Bouvier on September 12, 1953.

Religion: Roman Catholic.

Political party: Democratic.

Term of office: January 20, 1961 to November 22, 1963.

Died: November 22, 1963.

Sidelight: When John F. Kennedy was shot in the head by Lee Harvey Oswald he was only forty-six years old, the youngest president to die in office. He was the fourth president to be assassinated.

Which president was a speed-reader who could read 2,000 words per minute with 95 percent comprehension?
Jimmy Carter. In addition to all the reading of official documents he had to do while in the White House, he would often read three to four books a week. Dylan Thomas was his favorite poet.

Does the president receive a salary?
Most definitely. George Washington volunteered to serve for free, provided that Congress would pay his expenses. Congress (wisely, it turned out) voted instead that the president would be paid $25,000 per year.

Harry S Truman was the first president to receive a salary of $100,000. President Bush receives a salary of $200,000 per year, plus $50,000 in expenses. Those incomes are taxable. In addition, Mr. Bush receives $100,000 (tax free) for travel and entertainment. The president is also entitled to numerous retirement benefits.

What mountains in the United States are named in honor of presidents?

There have been quite a few mountains named in honor of presidents. Among them are: Mount Washington, Mount Adams, Mount Jefferson, Mount Lincoln, and Mount Madison, all in New Hampshire; Mount Jefferson in Oregon; Mount Lincoln in Colorado; Grant Mountain Range in Nevada; and Mount McKinley and Mount Kennedy in Alaska.

Who was the first president to take up golf as a serious form of recreation?

William Howard Taft. Of course, the United States has had quite a few other golfing presidents, such as Woodrow Wilson, Dwight David Eisenhower, John F. Kennedy, Richard M. Nixon, Gerald Ford, and George Bush. Lyndon Johnson golfed, but kept his scores a secret from the press. Woodrow Wilson once described the game of golf as, "an ineffectual attempt to put an elusive ball into an obscure hole with implements ill-adapted to the purpose."

Which president said, "Four fifths of all our troubles in this life would disappear if we would only sit down and keep still"?

Calvin Coolidge. No wonder we keep referring to him as "Silent Cal."

Which president's wife banned dancing, card-playing, and alcoholic beverages in the White House?

James Polk's wife, Sarah, who was a devout Presbyterian. Other wives who barred alcoholic beverages in the White House were Lucy Webb Hayes (sometimes known as "Lemonade Lucy," because she served lemonade at formal White House functions), Lucretia Garfield (she refused to serve wine at dinner), and Rosalynn Carter.

Which president proposed to his wife on their very first date?

Lyndon Baines Johnson. Claudia "Lady Bird" Alta Taylor married him two months later.

Lyndon Baines Johnson

36th President

Born: August 27, 1908, near Stonewall, Texas.

Father: Sam Ealy Johnson, Jr.

Mother: Rebekah Baines Johnson.

Married: Claudia "Lady Bird" Alta Taylor on November 17, 1934.

Religion: Disciples of Christ.

Political party: Democratic.

Term of office: November 22, 1963 to January 20, 1969.

Died: January 22, 1973.

Sidelight: LBJ was the first vice president to witness the assassination of the president whom he succeeded.

What terrible events have happened to presidents who have been elected every twenty years from 1840 to 1980?
Since 1840, there seems be a curse associated with presidents who have been elected every twenty years:

Election of 1840—William Henry Harrison died in office (1841)

Election of 1860—Lincoln was assassinated (1865)

Election of 1880—Garfield was assassinated (1881)

Election of 1900—McKinley was assassinated (1901)

Election of 1920—Harding died in office (1923)

Election of 1940—Franklin Roosevelt died in office (1945)

Election of 1960—Kennedy was assassinated (1963)

Election of 1980—Reagan was shot and nearly killed (1981)

Which future president at fifteen, ran away from home, journeying from Texas to California, where he found work as a grape picker and auto mechanic?
Lyndon Baines Johnson

When Richard M. Nixon resigned as the thirty-seventh president, to whom was the letter of resignation addressed and what did the letter say?

The letter was addressed to his secretary of state, Henry Kissinger. It read in full: "Dear Mr. Secretary: I hereby resign the office of the President of the United States. Sincerely, Richard M. Nixon."

Richard Nixon is the only U.S. president to resign from the office.

Richard Milhous Nixon

37th President

Born: January 9, 1913, in Yorba Linda, California.

Father: Francis Anthony Nixon.

Mother: Hannah Milhous Nixon.

Married: Thelma "Patricia" Catherine Ryan on June 21, 1940.

Religion: Quaker.

Political party: Republican.

Term of office: January 20, 1969 to August 9, 1974.

Sidelight: He was the first president to resign from the office.

Which president was so stubborn (bullheaded, some would say) that his opponents conferred upon him the sobriquet "His Obstinancy"?
Grover Cleveland. Once he made up his mind, it was difficult to get him to change his decision.

The wives of which presidents were deeply interested in astrology?
Nancy Reagan, who sometimes consulted with an astrologer to aid in scheduling presidential meetings, and Florence "Flossie" Harding, wife of Warren Harding. In 1920, Flossie Harding went to a woman called Madame Marcia, a popular Washington, D.C., psychic, to find out about the chances for her husband's Republican presidential nomination. Madame Marcia told Mrs. Harding that her husband, even though he was a dark-horse candidate, would win both the nomination and the election, but that he would suddenly die in office. Strangely enough, her predictions did come true.

Who was the first president to broadcast a speech over the radio?
Warren G. Harding. His speech at the dedication of the Francis Scott Key Memorial at Fort McHenry in Baltimore, Maryland, on June 14, 1922, was transmitted by radio station WEAR.

Who was the first person to become president by way of the twenty-fifth Amendment?

Gerald R. Ford. On August 9, 1974, taking over after Richard Nixon's resignation, Ford became the thirty-eighth president, although he was frequently referred to by members of Congress and by members of the press as "acting president."

Gerald Rudolph Ford

38th President

Born: July 14, 1913, in Omaha, Nebraska.

Father: Leslie Lynch King.

Mother: Dorothy Ayer Gardner King Ford.

Married: Elizabeth "Betty" Bloomer Warren on October 15, 1948.

Religion: Episcopalian.

Political party: Republican.

Term of office: August 9, 1974 to January 20, 1977.

Sidelight: Gerald Ford was the first vice president not elected by the people to become president. He became vice president when Nixon's elected vice president, Spiro Agnew, resigned.

We know the birthplaces of almost all the presidents, but there is one president whose birthplace is not definitely known. Which one?

Chester A. Arthur, who was president from 1881 to 1885. Because his family moved around so much, Arthur's birthplace is not absolutely certain. Some say he was born in Fairfield, Vermont. Others claim he was born in a log cabin in nearby Waterville, New York.

During Arthur's campaign and during his presidency, in fact, some of his political opponents claimed (without proof) that Arthur had been born in Canada, and, therefore, was ineligible to be president because of provisions in the Constitution. The courts have never decided whether the Constitutional requirement that a president must be a natural born citizen disqualifies a person born abroad to American parents.

How many presidents have been left-handed?

Three: Harry S Truman, Gerald R. Ford, and James A. Garfield.

Which president had the biggest feet?

Probably Warren G. Harding, who wore size fourteen shoes. Washington, however, with size thirteen boots, was not far behind.

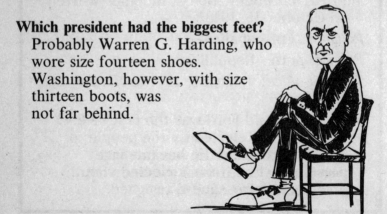

Who was president when the first gaslights were installed in the White House?

James K. Polk

Who was the first president to have been born in a hospital?

Jimmy Carter. All previous presidents had been born at home.

James Earl Carter, Jr.

39th President

Born: October 1, 1924, in Plains, Georgia.

Father: James Earl Carter.

Mother: Lillian Gordy Carter.

Married: Eleanor Rosalynn Smith on July 7, 1946.

Religion: Baptist.

Political party: Democratic.

Term of office: January 20, 1977 to January 20, 1981.

Sidelight: Jimmy Carter was the first president elected from the Deep South since before the Civil War.

What well-known American expression did Martin Van Buren popularize?

"O.K." During the election of 1840, when Harrison defeated Van Buren, the word "O.K." (because Van Buren hailed from Kinderhook, New York or, as it was sometimes referred to—Old Kinderhook,) began to crop up in speeches and print.

To support Van Buren's campaign, Old Kinderhook Clubs—or O.K. Clubs, as they were known—were formed. Shortly thereafter the expression "O.K." came to mean all right.

Which president claimed that his first childhood memory—at age four—was hearing that Abraham Lincoln had been elected president?

Woodrow Wilson claimed that hearing Lincoln had been elected president and that there was a war coming were his first childhood memories.

Who was the first president to have been divorced?
Ronald Reagan. He was married to motion picture star Jane Wyman from 1940 to 1948. After divorcing Ms. Wyman, Reagan married Nancy Davis, also an actress, in 1952. Nancy Davis can be seen in the movie *Donovan's Brain.*

Ronald Reagan

40th President

Born: February 6, 1911, in Tampico, Illinois.

Father: John Edward Reagan.

Mother: Nelle Wilson Reagan.

Married: Jane Wyman (first wife) on June 25, 1940, and Nancy Davis (second wife) on March 1, 1952.

Religion: Disciples of Christ.

Political party: Republican.

Term of office: January 20, 1981 to January 20, 1989.

Sidelight: He was, at age sixty-nine, the oldest person to be elected president.

Which early president was such a connoisseur of fine wines that during his two terms of office his wine bill exceeded $10,000?

Thomas Jefferson. Jefferson also encouraged Italian grape growers to settle in Virginia.

Have any members of a United States presidential ticket ever died before an election?

Yes. Republican William Taft's vice-presidential nominee, former New York congressman James Schoolcraft Sherman, who was Taft's vice president during his first administration, died from Bright's disease (a kidney ailment) one week before the 1912 election. He was replaced on the ticket by Nicholas Murray Butler.

Which future president, for a short time, was the youngest WWII pilot in the U.S. navy?

George Bush, who was commissioned as an ensign late in 1943, joined the new light aircraft carrier U.S.S. *San Jacinto* as a member of the Torpedo Bomber Squadron. Mr. Bush, then nineteen, was the youngest pilot at that time, and he saw quite a bit of hazardous action in the Pacific.

George Herbert Walker Bush

41st President

Born: June 12, 1924, in Milton, Massachusetts.

Father: Prescott Sheldon Bush.

Mother: Dorothy Walker Bush.

Married: Barbara Pierce on January 6, 1945.

Religion: Episcopalian.

Political party: Republican.

Term of office: January 20, 1989 to present.

Sidelight: When he attended the prestigious Phillips Academy in Andover, Massachusetts, his classmates nicknamed him "Poppy."

Which president was so afraid of electricity that he and his family frequently slept in the White House with all the lights burning?

Benjamin Harrison. It was during his term in 1891 in fact, that the Edison Company first installed electricity in the White House. Harrison and members of his family didn't understand electricity and did not wish to fool with it more than they absolutely had to. Their attitude was not uncommon at the time.

When George Bush played first base for Yale University's baseball team in 1947 and 1948, how did he do?

According to Jim Duffus, a former Yale pitcher, George Bush "wasn't the best ballplayer—but he was the leader." During his career, President Bush compiled a .251 batting average in 175 at bats.

George Bush's Baseball Career

A look at President George Bush's playing career at Yale University:
- ▶ **Height:** 6-0.   ▶ **Weight:** 170
- ▶ **Born:** Milton, Mass., June 12, 1924.
- ▶ **Bats:** Right.   ▶ **Throws:** Left.   ▶ **Position:** First base.

Year	G	AB	R	H	2B	3B	HR	RBI	SB	Avg.	Sig.	PO	A	E	Fid%
1947	26	88	16	21	2	0	1	9	5	.239	.295	252	11	7	.974
1948	25	87	15	23	6	2	1	14	2	.264	.414	190	13	2	.990
Totals	51	175	31	44	8	2	2	23	7	.251	.354	442	24	9	.981

What man—not even a candidate for the presidency—missed becoming president by just one vote?

Senator Ben Wade of Ohio. Had Andrew Johnson been impeached in 1867, Wade, as president of the Senate, would have been elevated to the presidency. The vote was as close as it could be. Impeachment required two thirds of the total votes cast, or at the time, thirty-six out of the fifty-four votes. Thirty-five senators voted for Johnson's removal, nineteen voted for his acquittal. Thus, President Johnson survived by one vote.

Which president experimented with breeding bison as a good source of meat?

George Washington. He conducted his experiments at Mount Vernon. He felt that bison meat would be cheaper than beef, and bison hardier than cattle.

117

Theodore Roosevelt lent his first name to what popular American toy?

The Teddy bear. It seems that when Teddy Roosevelt went big-game hunting in Africa in 1902, he came upon a bear cub trapped in a tree. Teddy saved the animal's life, and newspapers around the world played up the story. Soon children starting naming their stuffed toys Teddy and the Teddy bear was born.

Presidents of the United States

No.	Name	Life Dates	Politics	Place of Birth	Dates of Term
1	George Washington	1732–1799	Federalist	Virginia	1789–1797
2	John Adams	1735–1826	Federalist	Massachusetts	1797–1801
3	Thomas Jefferson	1743–1826	Dem.-Rep.	Virginia	1801–1809
4	James Madison	1751–1836	Dem.-Rep.	Virginia	1809–1817
5	James Monroe	1758–1831	Dem.-Rep.	Virginia	1817–1825
6	John Quincy Adams	1767–1848	Dem.-Rep.	Massachusetts	1825–1829
7	Andrew Jackson	1767–1845	Democrat	South Carolina	1829–1837
8	Martin Van Buren	1782–1862	Democrat	New York	1837–1841
9	William Henry Harrison	1773–1841	Whig	Virginia	1841
10	John Tyler	1790–1862	Democrat	Virginia	1841–1845
11	James Knox Polk	1795–1849	Democrat	North Carolina	1845–1849
12	Zachary Taylor	1784–1850	Whig	Virginia	1849–1850
13	Millard Fillmore	1800–1874	Whig	New York	1850–1853

Presidents of the United States
(cont.)

No.	Name	Life Dates	Politics	Place of Birth	Dates of Term
14	Franklin Pierce	1804–1869	Democrat	New Hampshire	1853–1857
15	James Buchanan	1791–1868	Democrat	Pennsylvania	1857–1861
16	Abraham Lincoln	1809–1865	Republican	Kentucky	1861–1865
17	Andrew Johnson	1808–1875	Republican	North Carolina	1865–1869
18	Ulysses Simpson Grant	1822–1885	Republican	Ohio	1869–1877
19	Rutherford Birchard Hayes	1822–1893	Republican	Ohio	1877–1881
20	James Abram Garfield	1831–1881	Republican	Ohio	1881
21	Chester Alan Arthur	1830–1886	Republican	Vermont	1881–1885
22	Grover Cleveland	1837–1908	Democrat	New Jersey	1885–1889
23	Benjamin Harrison	1833–1901	Republican	Ohio	1889–1893
24	Grover Cleveland	1837–1908	Democrat	New Jersey	1893–1897
25	William McKinley	1843–1901	Republican	Ohio	1897–1901

No.	Name	Life Dates	Politics	Place of Birth	Dates of Term
26	Theodore Roosevelt	1858–1919	Republican	New York	1901–1909
27	William Howard Taft	1857–1930	Republican	Ohio	1909–1913
28	Woodrow Wilson	1856–1924	Democrat	Virginia	1913–1921
29	Warren Gamaliel Harding	1865–1923	Republican	Ohio	1921–1923
30	Calvin Coolidge	1872–1933	Republican	Vermont	1923–1929
31	Herbert Clark Hoover	1874–1964	Republican	Iowa	1929–1933
32	Franklin Delano Roosevelt	1882–1945	Democrat	New York	1933–1945
33	Harry S Truman	1884–1972	Democrat	Missouri	1945–1953
34	Dwight David Eisenhower	1890–1969	Republican	Texas	1953–1961
35	John Fitzgerald Kennedy	1917–1963	Democrat	Massachusetts	1961–1963
36	Lyndon Baines Johnson	1908–1973	Democrat	Texas	1963–1969
37	Richard Milhous Nixon	1913–	Republican	California	1969–1974
38	Gerald Rudolph Ford	1913–	Republican	Nebraska	1974–1977
39	James Earl Carter, Jr.	1924–	Democrat	Georgia	1977–1981
40	Ronald Reagan	1911–	Republican	Illinois	1981–1989
41	George Herbert Walker Bush	1924–	Republican	Massachusetts	1989–

121

Vice Presidents of the United States

Name and (party)	Life Dates	Place of Birth	Dates of Term	President Served Under
1 John Adams (F)	1735–1826	Massachusetts	1789–1797	Washington
2 Thomas Jefferson (DR)	1743–1826	Virginia	1797–1801	J. Adams
3 Aaron Burr (DR)	1756–1836	New Jersey	1801–1805	Jefferson
4 George Clinton (DR)	1739–1812	New York	1805–1812	Jefferson and Madison
5 Elbridge Gerry (DR)	1744–1814	Massachusetts	1813–1814	Madison
6 Daniel D. Tompkins (DR)	1774–1825	New York	1817–1825	Monroe
7 John C. Calhoun	1782–1850	South Carolina	1825–1832	J. Q. Adams and Jackson
8 Martin Van Buren (D)	1782–1862	New York	1833–1837	Jackson
9 Richard M. Johnson (D)	1780–1850	Kentucky	1837–1841	Van Buren
10 John Tyler (W)	1790–1862	Virginia	1841	W. H. Harrison
11 George M. Dallas (D)	1792–1864	Pennsylvania	1845–1849	Polk
12 Millard Fillmore (W)	1800–1874	New York	1849–1850	Taylor
13 William R. King (D)	1786–1853	North Carolina	1853	Pierce
14 John C. Breckinridge (D)	1821–1875	Kentucky	1857–1861	Buchanan
15 Hannibal Hamlin (R)	1809–1891	Maine	1861–1865	Lincoln

Name and (party)	Life Dates	Place of Birth	Dates of Term	President Served Under
16 Andrew Johnson (U)	1808–1875	North Carolina	1865	Lincoln
17 Schuyler Colfax (R)	1823–1885	New York	1869–1873	Grant
18 Henry Wilson (R)	1812–1875	New Hampshire	1873–1875	Grant
19 William A. Wheeler (R)	1819–1887	New York	1877–1881	Hayes
20 Chester A. Arthur (R)	1830–1886	Vermont	1881	Garfield
21 Thomas A. Hendricks (D)	1819–1885	Ohio	1885	Cleveland
22 Levi P. Morton (R)	1824–1920	Vermont	1889–1893	B. Harrison
23 Adlai E. Stevenson (D)	1835–1914	Kentucky	1893–1897	Cleveland
24 Garrett A. Hobart (R)	1844–1899	New Jersey	1897–1899	McKinley
25 Theodore Roosevelt (R)	1858–1919	New York	1901	McKinley
26 Charles W. Fairbanks (R)	1852–1918	Ohio	1905–1909	T. Roosevelt
27 James S. Sherman (R)	1855–1912	New York	1909–1912	Taft
28 Thomas R. Marshall (D)	1854–1925	Indiana	1913–1921	Wilson
29 Calvin Coolidge (R)	1872–1933	Vermont	1921–1923	Harding
30 Charles G. Dawes (R)	1865–1951	Ohio	1925–1929	Coolidge

F = Federalist   DR = Democrat-Republican   W = Whig   D = Democrat   R = Republican   U = Unaffiliated

Note: Andrew Johnson was a Democrat nominated by Republicans and elected with Lincoln on the National Union Ticket.

Vice Presidents of the United States
(cont.)

	Name and (party)	Life Dates	Place of Birth	Dates of Term	President Served Under
31	Charles Curtis (R)	1860–1936	Kansas	1929–1933	Hoover
32	John N. Garner (D)	1868–1967	Texas	1933–1941	F. D. Roosevelt
33	Henry A. Wallace (D)	1888–1965	Iowa	1941–1945	F. D. Roosevelt
34	Harry S Truman (D)	1884–1972	Missouri	1945	F. D. Roosevelt
35	Alben W. Barkley (D)	1877–1956	Kentucky	1949–1953	Truman
36	Richard M. Nixon (R)	1913–	California	1953–1961	Eisenhower
37	Lyndon B. Johnson (D)	1908–1973	Texas	1961–1963	Kennedy
38	Hubert H. Humphrey (D)	1911–1978	South Dakota	1965–1969	Johnson
39	Spiro T. Agnew (R)	1918–	Maryland	1969–1973	Nixon
40	Gerald R. Ford (R)	1913–	Nebraska	1973–1974	Nixon
41	Nelson A. Rockefeller (R)	1908–1979	Maine	1974–1977	Ford
42	Walter F. Mondale (D)	1928–	Minnesota	1977–1981	Carter
43	George Bush (R)	1924–	Massachusetts	1981–1989	Reagan
44	J. Danforth Quayle (R)	1947–	Indiana	1989–	Bush

F = Federalist   DR = Democrat-Republican   W = Whig   D = Democrat   R = Republican   U = Unaffiliated

First Ladies

President	Wife's Name	Year and Place of Wife's Birth	Married	Wife Died
Washington	Martha Dandridge Custis	1732, Virginia	1759	1802
John Adams	Abigail Smith	1744, Massachusetts	1764	1818
Jefferson	Martha Wayles Skelton	1748, Virginia	1772	1782
Madison	Dorothea "Dolley" Payne Todd	1768, North Carolina	1794	1849
Monroe	Elizabeth "Eliza" Kortright	1768, New York	1786	1830
J. Q. Adams	Louisa Catherine Johnson	1775, England	1797	1852
Jackson	Mrs. Rachel Donelson Robards	1767, Virginia	1791	1828
Van Buren	Hannah Hoes	1783, New York	1807	1819
W. H. Harrison	Anna Symmes	1775, New Jersey	1795	1864
Tyler	Letitia Christian	1790, Virginia	1813	1842
	Julia Gardiner	1820, New York	1844	1889
Polk	Sarah Childress	1803, Tennessee	1824	1891
Taylor	Margaret Smith	1788, Maryland	1810	1852
Fillmore	Abigail Powers	1798, New York	1826	1853

125

First Ladies
(cont.)

President	Wife's Name	Year and Place of Wife's Birth	Married	Wife Died
Pierce	Caroline Carmichael McIntosh	1813, New Jersey	1858	1881
Buchanan	Jane Means Appleton	1806, New Hampshire	1834	1863
	(unmarried)	—	—	—
Lincoln	Mary Todd	1818, Kentucky	1842	1882
A. Johnson	Eliza McCardle	1810, Tennessee	1827	1876
Grant	Julia Dent	1826, Missouri	1848	1902
Hayes	Lucy Ware Webb	1831, Ohio	1852	1889
Garfield	Lucretia Rudolph	1832, Ohio	1858	1918
Arthur	Ellen Lewis Herndon	1837, Virginia	1859	1880
Cleveland	Frances Folsom	1864, New York	1886	1947
B. Harrison	Caroline Lavinia Scott	1832, Ohio	1853	1892
	Mary Scott Lord Dimmick	1858, Pennsylvania	1896	1948
McKinley	Ida Saxton	1847, Ohio	1871	1907
T. Roosevelt	Alice Hathaway Lee	1861, Massachusetts	1880	1884
	Edith Kermit Carow	1861, Connecticut	1886	1948

President	Wife's Name	Year and Place of Wife's Birth	Married	Wife Died
Taft	Helen Herron	1861, Ohio	1886	1943
Wilson	Ellen Louise Axson	1860, Georgia	1885	1914
	Edith Bolling Gait	1872, Virginia	1915	1961
Harding	Florence Kling De Wolfe	1860, Ohio	1891	1924
Coolidge	Grace Anna Goodhue	1879, Vermont	1905	1957
Hoover	Lou Henry	1875, Iowa	1899	1944
F. D. Roosevelt	Anna Eleanor Roosevelt	1884, New York	1905	1962
Truman	Bess Wallace	1885, Missouri	1919	1982
Eisenhower	Mamie Geneva Doud	1896, Iowa	1916	1979
Kennedy	Jacqueline Lee Bouvier	1929, New York	1953	—
L. B. Johnson	Claudia "Lady Bird" Alta Taylor	1912, Texas	1934	—
Nixon	Thelma Catherine Patricia Ryan	1912, Nevada	1940	—
Ford	Elizabeth "Betty" Bloomer Warren	1918, Illinois	1948	—
Carter	Rosalynn Smith	1928, Georgia	1946	—
Reagan	Jane Wyman	1914, Missouri	1940	—
	Nancy Davis	1921 (?), New York	1952	—
Bush	Barbara Pierce	1925, New York	1945	—

127

Presidential and Vice Presidential Nominees

	Democratic		Republican	
Year	President	Vice President	President	Vice President
1844	James K. Polk*	George M. Dallas	Henry Clay (Whig)	Theo. Frelinghuysen
1848	Lewis Cass	William Butler	Zachary Taylor* (Whig)	Millard Fillmore
1852	Franklin Pierce*	William King	Winfield Scott (Whig)	William Graham
1856	James Buchanan*	John Breckinridge	John Freemont	William Dayton
1860	John Breckinridge	Joseph Lane	Abraham Lincoln*	Hannibal Hamlin
1864	George McClellan	G.H. Pendleton	Abraham Lincoln*	Andrew Johnson
1868	Horatio Seymour	Francis Blair	Ulysses S. Grant*	Schuyler Colfax
1872	Horace Greeley	B. Gratz Brown	Ulysses S. Grant*	Henry Wilson
1876	Samuel J. Tilden	Thomas Hendricks	Rutherford B. Hayes*	William Wheeler
1880	Winfield Hancock	William English	James A. Garfield*	Chester A. Arthur
1884	Grover Cleveland*	Thomas Hendricks	James Blaine	John Logan
1888	Grover Cleveland	A.G. Thurman	Benjamin Harrison*	Levi Morton
1892	Grover Cleveland*	Adlai Stevenson	Benjamin Harrison	Whitelaw Reid

Year	Democratic President	Vice President	Republican President	Vice President
1896	William J. Bryan	Adlai Stevenson	William McKinley*	Garret Hobart
1900	William J. Bryan	Adlai Stevenson	William McKinley*	Theodore Roosevelt
1904	Alton Parker	Henry Davis	Theodore Roosevelt*	Charles Fairbanks
1908	William J. Bryan	John Kern	William H. Taft*	James Sherman
1912	Woodrow Wilson*	Thomas Marshall	William H. Taft	James Sherman (1)
1916	Woodrow Wilson*	Thomas Marshall	Charles Hughes	Charles Fairbanks
1920	James M. Cox	Franklin D. Roosevelt	Warren G. Harding*	Calvin Coolidge
1924	John W. Davis	Charles W. Bryan	Calvin Coolidge*	Charles G. Dawes
1928	Alfred E. Smith	Joseph T. Robinson	Herbert Hoover*	Charles Curtis
1932	Franklin D. Roosevelt*	John N. Garner	Herbert Hoover	Charles Curtis
1936	Franklin D. Roosevelt*	John N. Garner	Alfred M. Landon	Frank Knox
1940	Franklin D. Roosevelt*	Henry A. Wallace	Wendell L. Willkie	Charles McNary
1944	Franklin D. Roosevelt*	Harry S Truman	Thomas E. Dewey	John W. Bricker
1948	Harry S Truman*	Alben W. Barkley	Thomas E. Dewey	Earl Warren

Asterisk (*) denotes winning ticket

(1) Died Oct. 30; replaced on ballot by Nicholas Butler.

Presidential and Vice Presidential Nominees
(cont.)

Year	Democratic		Republican	
	President	Vice President	President	Vice President
1952	Adlai E. Stevenson	John J. Sparkman	Dwight D. Eisenhower*	Richard M. Nixon
1956	Adlai E. Stevenson	Estes Kefauver	Dwight D. Eisenhower*	Richard M. Nixon
1960	John F. Kennedy*	Lyndon B. Johnson	Richard M. Nixon	Henry Cabot Lodge
1964	Lyndon B. Johnson*	Hubert H. Humphrey	Barry M. Goldwater	William E. Miller
1968	Hubert H. Humphrey	Edmund S. Muskie	Richard M. Nixon*	Spiro T. Agnew
1972	George S. McGovern	R. Sargent Shriver Jr.	Richard M. Nixon*	Spiro T. Agnew
1976	Jimmy Carter*	Walter F. Mondale	Gerald R. Ford	Robert J. Dole
1980	Jimmy Carter	Walter F. Mondale	Ronald Reagan*	George Bush
1984	Walter F. Mondale	Geraldine Ferraro	Ronald Reagan*	George Bush
1988	Michael S. Dukakis	Lloyd Bentsen	George Bush*	J. Danforth Quayle

Asterisk (*) denotes winning ticket

CAMELOT WORLD
A FRESH LOOK
AT OUR WORLD

STRANGER THAN FICTION

by MELVIN BERGER

ASTOUND YOUR FRIENDS
WITH INCREDIBLE, LITTLE-KNOWN FACTS ABOUT...

KILLER BUGS   76036-3/$2.95 US/$3.50 Can

More people are killed by insects than by all other animals combined—including sharks and snakes.

DINOSAURS   76052-5/$2.95 US/$3.50 Can

Dinosaurs are the largest, most magnificent and most terrifying creatures that ever roamed the Earth.

MONSTERS   76053-3/$2.95 US/$3.50 Can

Do creatures like Big Foot and the Abominable Snowman really exist?

SEA MONSTERS   76054-1/$2.95 US/$3.50 Can

Unlike the shark in *Jaws*, this book is about the real living sea monsters that swim the waters of the world.

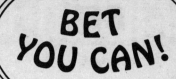